LIVING WATERS PRAYER LETTERS

BY LYNNE C. GRANGER

Living Waters Prayer Letters

by Lynne C. Granger

Printed in the United States of America.

Edited by Xulon Press

ISBN 9781498434881

www.xulonpress.com

Dedication

To my Lord and Savior who holds me in the palm of His hand,
and leads me daily by His Holy Spirit.

Acknowledgments

Love always to our Lord and Savior Jesus Christ!

I am thankful for my wonderful Christian and accomplished family and for the love of my life, Jerry.

I want to thank all my readers of the e-mails these past six years and Jodi Cole from Calvin College.

My gratitude is always to my extraordinary publishing team who embarked on this remarkable journey with me.

They include Lydia Granger; Kate Luce, assistant editor; Bill Coté, Ph.D., editor; photographer and friend Rod Gleason, and our publisher Xulon Press.

You all have been a continuous blessing in my life.

Editor's Preface

Launching yourself into the college years is an adventure filled with wonder, excitement and hope. It also may be fraught with doubt, pain and confusion. Lynne Granger remembers those years acutely and how the Lord helped her through them day by day and how He continues to light her path now and toward the future. This book is a collection of inspired e-mails Lynne sent over the past six years to her many grandchildren, nieces and nephews as they plunged into college.

Lynne often would be prodded awake at perhaps 4 or 5 a.m. with a message from the Lord and would rush to her desk or computer to capture the flow from above. Many of the messages are inspired by the rhythms of her life as an artist, singer and musician. Other times she focuses on what happened to her when she came to know the Lord at age fourteen, rescuing her from an often-tumultuous childhood and youth. Still other messages hinge on how she copes with her life as a wife, mother, grandmother and Christian friend.

It's not that her own life has been so easy. She sometimes notes in a letter how one of her painful illnesses is striking her again and what she's doing, with God's help, to climb above it all.

Her son, Todd Granger, says he thinks two things define his mother's legacy: "First is that she's a prayer warrior for others. Second is her response to her own physical troubles for forty years. She never blames God. I don't think I've ever heard her say, 'Oh, why is He doing this to me?' She simply accepts it and moves on. Her faithfulness is to God's plan."

In the original e-mails she often mentions her young recipients by name, but virtually all of those references have been removed from this collection to protect students' privacy. Lynne chose, however, to have Lydia Granger, her eighteen-year-old niece, write the foreword. Lydia's heartfelt words set the scene for young readers for all the letters to come.

After Lynne's letters, assistant editor Kate Luce highlights in "One More Note" her own story of how reliance on God equips young people with the strength and comfort they need to tackle life's challenges and opportunities once they are out of college.

The students did not receive the seven paintings printed in the book, but Lynne includes them here to reflect in glowing and powerful colors and tones the artwork that so often was and is in her mind as she writes the dispatches. She's confident that those, too, come from the Lord.

The e-mails were directed to college students, but we think the book may trigger a responsive chord in the minds and hearts of many a parent, grandparent or friend who is searching for some written wisdom to hand off to their favorite young adult.

On a personal note I am honored to be editor of Lynne Granger's book. Lynne and her husband, Jerry, are dear friends, as they were for my late wife, Donna Coté. I know Donna, who sometimes heard and perhaps even saw the Holy Spirit, would say "Hallelujah!" about this book, as I do. Amen.

—William E. Coté, Ph.D.

Foreword

*G*od can. God can bond people through their love of hydrangeas and well-kept gardens. God can spark joy through a fresh piano song. God can place hurting people together and help them gain strength from one another through their prayers. God can stop what you're doing and direct you toward something better. God can cause family to be neighbors, to be friends, to be collaborators. *God can, and God has.* This is our story—my dear aunt Lynne, God and me. God can and will in your life.

These journals, prayers and lessons have been compiled to stir up inspiration and spur on the desire to be in greater contact with our Father. Lynne writes from the heart, whether it is her personal cry for healing or sharing what she's been learning in her quiet times. These are her stories, and she willingly shares them with you so you may know more of His goodness.

But do not be content with these pages. Get on your knees, speak up in your classroom, direct intentional conversations, and you will be overwhelmed with your own revelations and the outpouring of God's love. Go out and discover for yourself that *God can*.

In all His love,
Lydia Mae Granger

Living Waters–Introduction

"He that believeth on me, as the scripture hath said, out of his belly
shall flow rivers of living water."
John 7:38 (KJV)

As a certified scuba diver, I have been in waters from the North
Sea to Venezuela. I have seen cold and dead water and bright,
inhabited living water.

When coral is lifeless it has no color, but waters with life are
colorful, with an abundance of living organisms, as in a healthy
ecosystem.

From this experience I have drawn the verse, "He that believeth
on me, as the scripture hath said, out of his belly shall flow rivers of
living water" (John 7:38, KJV). This is my premise for *Living Waters
Prayer Letters*.

Since I was fourteen years old I have known what I wanted to
do with my life. And now that I am seventy-four, God has proven
Himself worthy. I feel more confident.

By the time our family started going to college, I started writing
letters called *College Kids*. Knowing their immediate question,
"What am I supposed to be doing with my life?" I have pulled out
many words and readings to answer this age-long search. Scripture,
of course, has been at the top of my list for answers.

God has brought me down a unique path. First, I was an abused
child. Then my life radically changed when I met a wonderful

Christian man who became my friend and husband. I started my Christian musical endeavors and became a mom of four. I was diagnosed as bi-polar at age sixty. Later in life I became an artist and now an author of my first book *Living Waters Prayer Letters*.

I am filled with great enthusiasm, as our team has come together to glorify our great God and listen to His Word.

For six years I have ministered to college students, starting with a host of grandchildren, nieces and nephews, scholarship recipients and friends. As a way to continue to bless and minister to students, all proceeds of this book will go to support Christian education.

I broke my leg last summer, and still wanting to serve God I took inventory. I had my right arm and my brain, thanks be to God. He then enlarged this college ministry based on God's Word to include you, the reader. Thus a book, *Living Waters Prayer Letters,* was born.

It was said, "I didn't know Lynne could write," and her reply was, "She didn't know either!" I come to you in love and the presence of the Holy Spirit. So let's walk hand-in-hand studying and being challenged and praying through the selected scriptures and letters. Let us drink of the Living Water and be satisfied. "To Him be the glory and dominion forever and ever" (1 Peter 5:11, NKJV).

—Lynne Granger
LivingWaterPrayerLetters@gmail.com

Photo by Dr. Robert Kribs, fellow sailor

Opening Letter

"In all your ways submit to Him, and He will make your paths straight."
Proverbs 3:6 (NIV)

God, I am so blessed and I thank You for my friend and editor Bill Coté. I remember the day he called announcing we could move on to the next step with this devotional book with the publisher Xulon. Originally I thought it would take two weeks to bring everything to the table. But it took longer—months.

God has given me a vision and a heart for young people. The college years are different from any other time in one's life. The students get a demanding new schedule each semester, and it is theirs to manage one hundred percent on their own. "Show me your ways, Lord; teach me your paths" (Psalm 25:4, NIV).

These devotionals are intended to help students (and readers of all ages) to deepen their walk with Jesus during pivotal years and to help them connect the Bible to the struggles, hopes, dreams and decisions they face. College is the beginning of a journey that lasts a lifetime—and who better to help than Christ at the helm?

As a grandma, aunt and friend, I pray these young people connect to God not only nine but twelve months of the year and seven days a week.

We have a saying in our family. . .*God speed.*

Love always,
Grandma, Aunt Lynne and friend

College Kids

"You can pray for anything, and if you have faith, you will receive it."
Matthew 21:22 (NLT)

Welcome to College Kids! This new year I have done a lot of studying and praying, and by the Holy Spirit I would like to share so we can grow together. We will be studying numerous topics.

As you walk with God, "He will never leave you nor forsake you" (Deuteronomy 31:6, NIV). No matter what is going on in your life you can claim this promise. The greatest gift is love, not fear. He promises us a sound mind (2 Timothy 1:7, KJV), so pray, pray, pray, for yourselves and others.

Didn't Christ reach out and touch you? If not, ask Christ into your life.

Ask Him into your heart to forgive your sins. Ask God to direct your path and show you His perfect plan for your life. Now receive eternal life, a free gift, and ask God to fill you with His Holy Spirit so He will give you power to enable you to reach others to bless them, and they will in turn bless you.

Challenge: There are a lot of "asks" in the above paragraph, but it is true that if you don't ask you don't get. So be it!

Prayer: Let this be the first day of my life because I am asking!

Love always,
Grandma, Aunt Lynne and friend

Choices

"I have set before you life and death, blessings and curses.
Now choose life."
Deuteronomy 30:19 (NIV)

Today is a new day of choices. I can choose joy the minute I open my eyes, and I can choose to go to church with my family and cousins.

God is committed to your choice of improvement and committed to your perfection and betterment. He will leave behind your sin and imperfections—just ask. The choice is renewal or stagnation. I have had to learn how to change because of childhood insecurities, but now through growth and lots of prayer I welcome change more than ever and have found new passions in life—love for people. Remember God is in control—His steps are ours.

I prayed for you
That learning will be a joy
That you will have clarity of mind
Abandonment of fear
Ability to concentrate and recollect what you have learned
And the ability to apply it to your life.
Enjoy the challenge, take one step at a time. . .
Jesus is with you one step at a time.
Remember: there are only His steps in the sand for He is carrying you.

I bless you that you will know His presence and His guidance. May His peace be with you, and may reading *Living Waters Prayer Letters* fill you with renewal and restoration.

Challenge: I choose to honor You, God, with obedience.

Prayer: Help me to keep my commitment and the promise of joy.

Love always,
Grandma, Aunt Lynne and friend

The Name of Jesus

"For God so loved the world that he gave his only begotten Son,
that whoever believes in him shall not perish but have eternal life."
John 3:16 (NASB)

*J*esus. His name has been and will be important for all time. Our names are important because God calls us by name to come follow Him, to take up the cross and walk daily with Him. We need to believe in the name of Jesus, God's one and only Son, because this is power and life.

I did not feel love from my earthly father in my earlier years. My best friend, Joyce, told me how great the love of the heavenly Father is, so I chose to look for the perfect love in Him. Praise the Lord!

Once we call on His name and experience the love of the perfect Father, that love is abundant and can overflow onto those around us.

We received a personal letter from Youth for Christ national president Dan Wolgemuth, and he said, "Now it is time to preach the gospel around us and to the places who have never heard of Him. New places with broken and lost kids. This is what God has called us to do. You propel us to these neighborhoods, into these relationships. For the least, for the lost." [1]

Challenge: Speak His name; He has power to lift you up and make you whole. Calling on Jesus by name can set us free to be the people God wants us to be. *I have come that you might have life abundantly* (John 10:10, NASB, paraphrased). I pray that you will call on Jesus in conversation and in your home—*lead on!*

Prayer: "Come; I say, come! Here I am, Lord. Touch and make me whole; heal me."

Love always,
Grandma, Aunt Lynne and friend

Faith Stories

"Know therefore that the Lord your God is God; he is the faithful God,
keeping his covenant of love to a thousand generations of those who
love him and keep his commandments."
Deuteronomy 7:9 (NIV)

D earest grandparents and those of this era, we each need to remember the defining moment when accepting Jesus Christ into our lives changed our hearts and minds forever. Our passion and emotions for the gospel define our love story with God, and we need to share it in a compelling manner. This hope for sharing *our* story is a continuing process. Have you shared your encounters with your loved ones so they are drawn to the life-changing message of Jesus Christ?

The current generation no longer knows our faith stories, even though they are familiar with the Bible stories. We need to share our life stories in our homes and everyday encounters, not just in the church. It is imperative that we share how Jesus Christ makes a continual difference in our daily lives and how we are seen as Christ's active witnesses in the world.

In other words, Grandpas and Grandmas, step up to the plate! It is not too late to share how God has changed you to affect one thousand generations.

Challenge: Make a point to schedule a time with your grandchild. They want to hear your story. So let God speak through you.

Prayer: Lead me to my calendar so I will make this happen. I know You will use me, so I will make myself available. Help me to be humble so that my grandchild and I will feed on the Word of God together.

Love always,
Grandma, Aunt Lynne and friend

Be Strong!

"Say to those with fearful hearts, 'Be strong, do not fear;
your God will come.'"
Isaiah 35:4 (NIV)

E verything is put away; books have been purchased, and you have seen your friends. Now it's time to settle down and choose the road you're meant to follow. This is not always easy. Have you chosen Christ as the Lord of your life and guide? You are going to learn how to put your trust in Him because He will lead you on the right road, which will bring you confidence and enthusiasm in your life.

Continue to remember Psalm 46:10: "Be still, and know I am God" (ESV). God is always an enabler and will guide you to the place you long for. "I will guide you along the best pathway for your life. I will advise you and watch over you" (Psalm 32:8, NLT).

Challenge: Continue to place your hopes in Him because God loves and cares for you deeply. Remember He came to give you life abundantly.

Prayer: Let God be your guide, not fear. The word for me this year is hope. It is amazing what happens when you put your hope in God.

Love always,
Grandma, Aunt Lynne and friend

Using Your Talents

"Do not neglect the gift that is in you."
1 Timothy 4:14 (ISV)

God set your DNA and placed your talents throughout your whole life. For me, my set of opportunities has centered on three themes: music, art and writing.

He knew what He was doing when He gave you a unique set of talents and opportunities. Now the question is, are you going to use these talents or not? You must not be distracted, but instead be watchful for temptations that would lead you astray. You all have blessings.

If you are sincerely interested in building a career around the talents God has given you, don't try to build a career around the talents you wish He had given you. Don't worry. He will provide the unique opportunities and tools you need. He wants you to be happy.

Challenge: Value the talents God has given you. Remember to thank Him and use these gifts to serve Him and others. Be a good steward. "You are the only person on earth who can use your ability." —Zig Ziglar

Prayer: God, help me to be all that You have enabled me to be and to be happy about it.

Love always,
Grandma, Aunt Lynne, friend

From My Heart

"Come to me, all you who are weary and burdened,
and I will give you rest."
Matthew 11:28 (NIV)

I remember when I was in Florida and had a particularly hard time with asthma and a persistent deep cough. I lay down and noticed I was full of fear and not calm. I realized I was self-consumed and not praying for others. I started praying, and it was like a kick-start, and the Bible verses started coming. Yeah—power!

Jesus is "the way, the truth, and the light: no man cometh to the Father, but by me" (John 14:6, KJV).

Do not be afraid; be still for a minute. Listen and watch what God is doing for you. He loves you and is your heavenly Father. Your job is simply to maintain your peace and remain faithful.

Challenge: In troubled times stay calm; do not fear, and do not worry. Try to get your emotions under control so you can again think clearly, act wisely and pray in faith. Remember to love God today and seek His presence.

Prayer: God, help me to love You daily and not fear for the morrow.

Always on the front lines,
Grandma, Aunt Lynne and friend

His Yoke Is Light

"Take my yoke upon you and learn from me, for I am gentle and humble
in heart, and you will find rest for your souls. For my yoke
is easy and my burden is light."
Matthew 11:29-30 (NIV)

S tewardship is an act of love to take care of something. The dictionary defines stewardship as *the careful and responsible management of something entrusted to one's care* [2].

A strange paradox occurs in our lives when we accept the heavy yoke of Christ—*all* our burdens become lighter. As we accept complete stewardship and give all we have and are to the kingdom cause, we become rich. When taking on the weighty responsibility of spreading the good news, we are able to simultaneously lighten our hearts and burdens before God.

At the very heart of Christian stewardship are acts of service, even at a great cost. But the wonderful thing is that Christian service does something to the server as well as to those we serve. As Christians, we are to receive God's gifts gratefully, cultivate responsibility and share them lovingly.

Challenge: What would others put as priority in life? I advise having a mentor to keep you focused on what is truly important. Write your priorities down. Record them so you can carry on while being reminded when life gets busy or complicated. Also, remember that God wants to be your number one priority! Your list of other priorities of family, job and the like only come second to Him. God always desires to be part of *all* parts of your life.

Prayer: Free me, Jesus, from these heavy burdens. Please love, heal and give me peace with God and help me to have spiritual productivity and purpose.

Love always,
Grandma, Aunt Lynne and friend

Pray for One Another

"I call on the Lord in my distress, and He answers me."
Psalm 120:1 (NIV)

Even though you find yourselves miles apart, what can you do for your neighbor? As Jesus reached out to us, let us reach out to each other. Remember to reach out in your pain, and joy will follow.

God is calling you for a special service. Start with what you have, and God will multiply your blessings and gifts, as a little seed in the ground can bring forth a harvest.

This is your moment to honor God with your commitment by praying for one another. Dream big and grow spiritually. The world is not so big, after all.

God bless each and every one. All of you are like a tapestry that shines eternally. Yes, you are in my heart and prayers. You are great because He is! Together we stand.

Challenge: Are you ready for special service? It is always good to think of others to have a full and meaningful life.

Prayer: Give me assurance and hope in Your protection day and night, God. I grow closer and honor You with my life.

Love always,
Grandma, Aunt Lynne and friend

A Chance to Start Over

*"Put on the new self, created to be like God in the
true righteousness and holiness."
Ephesians 4:24 (NIV)*

T he old has passed; the new day is here! You do not have to be
shackled by the past when God has your future already planned.
This is the powerful message of Christianity.

Watchman Nee said that "the path of every Christian has been
clearly marked out by God, and it is of supreme importance that each
one should know and walk in the God-appointed course" [3].

When we decide to accept Christ's gift of salvation, it is both a
one-time decision and a conscious daily commitment. We will put
on the new nature, head in the new direction and have the new way
of thinking the Holy Spirit gives.

Challenge: Face today with joyful anticipation. This is your opportunity, so do not let it slip away. Be steadfast with your decision to
follow Christ now and daily.

Prayer: God, help me to start today and build a powerful tomorrow!

Love always,
Grandma, Aunt Lynne and friend

The Warrior's Hand

"In everything give thanks; for this is God's will for you in Christ Jesus."
1 Thessalonians 5:18 (NASB)

I n church I was looking at my scarred and bruised hands, ashamed and thinking, *I should cover them!* All of a sudden, I started remembering Jesus' scarred and tormented hands on the cross. He was obedient to the suffering He endured, and I should be also. I started remembering the times when my hands had honored and blessed me. I began to praise Him joyfully in all circumstances, for this is the will of God for those who belong to Christ Jesus.

I prayerfully tried not to remember wounds of the past but the good of the present. Precious memories of my mother's and grand-mother's soft touches on my shoulder as well as those of neighbors and friends warmed me. The life-changing hands of Jesus touched me, and I said yes. I have said yes to enduring both the good and the bad, as Jesus did. I have said yes to giving thanks in all circum-stances. My hands touch my family and friends as I am able to bless them with the power of the Holy Spirit and the presence of Jesus. I am able to caress them with the hands of love, and I have been able to touch many shoulders with God's blessing. These hands have directed choirs, played guitar, expressed the meaning of solos and taught the love of God through music. This has prepared me for the large sweep of my hands through art.

Now, in this new chapter, I use my hands to write what God puts on my heart. His cross was and is always first. No person is beyond the loving touch of the Almighty. "For the Son of Man has come to seek and to save that which was lost" (Luke 19:10, NASB). We can honor God by helping those and ourselves in need, through Him, with our hands. It is a continuous process.

Now my hands are those of a warrior, God's warrior. I am now no longer ashamed of their looks. My husband reminds me that my hands work, thus my first book *Living Waters*. On television, evangelist Robert Schuler often said, "Turn your scars into stars."

Challenge: Reach out and touch someone in need, and you will feel blessed.

Prayer: Have you received the hand, the touch of Jesus? "Touch me, Jesus; I am Yours." Make this a conscious decision today.

Love always, as I reach out and touch your shoulder,
Grandmother, Aunt Lynne and friend

Your Joy Shall Be Made Full

"The joy of the Lord is your strength."
Nehemiah 8:10 (NIV)

How long are we supposed to have a smile on our faces? As long as people treat us kindly or things are going well?

When dark clouds are overhead, remember that right above those dark clouds the sun is always shining. Clouds will not last forever, and the sun will shine in your life once again.

In the meantime, keep your joy. "He causes his sun to rise on the evil and the good, and sends rain on the righteous and the unrighteous" (Matthew 5:45, NIV).

As your strength is dissipated, you can keep your joy by knowing that on the other side of each test is promotion. On every side of every setback is opportunity, and then there is growth.

Just keep reminding yourself, *even though this is hard, even though I don't understand it, even though it's not fair, I'll keep a good attitude and have joy because God will bring me through, even in a better position.*

College students and grads, I have really prayed about this message, as it is timeless and timely. You are all in my heart, and I pray for you with great longing. God is real and has you in the palm of His hand in your joys and struggles.

God be with you as you continue to seek His will for your life. You will someday be a compass for others.

Challenge: "Ask and you will receive, that your joy may be full" (John 16:24, ESV).

Prayer: Come, Lord Jesus, and may Your joy be my strength as You light my path each and every day.

Love always,
Grandma, Aunt Lynne and friend

My Story

"And this same God who takes care of me will supply all your needs from
his glorious riches, which have been given to us in Christ Jesus.
Now all glory to God our Father forever and ever!"
Philippians 4:19-20 (NLT)

I cannot claim glory, but I thank You, God, for gathering all of my
experiences, both the good and the bad, to help me communicate
Your life-changing message of Jesus Christ to the world. You have
used my dark youth and changed my life at age fourteen through
Youth for Christ and my dear friend Joyce. You then filled me with
light and helped me each step of the way. In one of those steps, as
You shed Your light on me, You said, "The bonds and the chains from
generations before you are now broken." Now, in the name of Jesus,
thank You because my life has been unbelievable and I am thankful!
Your love, God, is awesome.

You took all of me and my experiences. Even my college music
education has given me form and order for my writing—just as in
music you begin with a phrase, then develop it and then come to the
culmination, enlightenment, recapitulation and, of course, the beat,
which has given me the innate ability to know where the commas
go. I never read a book until I was twenty-three years old, and I had
only one class in college outside of my major, and it was not writing.
It's been quite a ride.

Challenge: Jesus guard my heart, and as I offer you each day I will
say, "Thank You!"

Prayer: I love You so much, Lord Jesus, and again I make a commitment to follow You even more, right now.

Love always,
Grandma, Aunt Lynne and friend

29

As He Pleases

"Strengthen the feeble hands, steady the knees that give way; say to those with fearful hearts, 'Be strong, do not fear; your God will come....' Then will the lame leap like a deer, and the mute tongue shout for joy."
Isaiah 35:3-4, 6 (NIV)

In the last four years I have had orthopedic knee surgery, a broken right ankle and a knee replacement, and three weeks ago I broke my right leg. "It's time to pray," I told myself and then went to multiple doctors. The first orthopedic doctor told me my leg had healed in two weeks. The second orthopedic doctor told me my right knee did not need to be replaced. Amen!

Isaiah 35 speaks on the joy of the redeemed:

Then will the eyes of the blind be opened and the ears of the deaf unstopped. Then will the lame leap like a deer, and the mute tongue shout for joy   (Isaiah 35:5-6, NIV).

Shalom means "the way things ought to be." God is a God of relationships, and we are His. Yet we ache for that time and place when all will be right. Aching means we take seriously the implications of our faith in all we do.

Challenge: Read all of Isaiah 35, and you will find your joyful vocation—to love God, to care for that which God loves and to seek shalom.

Prayer: It's hard to be disciplined, but help me to be so I can be an example and have responsibility to my friends as we are living for Christ.

Love always,
Grandma, Aunt Lynne and friend

Foundation

"See what great love the Father has lavished on us, that we should be
called children of God! And that is what we are! The reason the world
does not know us is that it did not know him."
1 John 3:1 (NIV)

God has come to set us free. Get up! Let's learn the Word of
God. How are you going to understand the Bible if you don't
read it? Learn how to study the Bible; the professors are here to help
you. Take one thing you understand and run with it, then another and
another. This strong foundation is like building a house on a rock;
when the wind and storms come it will not fall.

Let the Holy Spirit renew your mind. What are you going to think
about today? What are your thoughts about people and yourself? You
do have choices!

He is the one life that sets you free, free from the turmoil and the
unknown. "I have come that they may have life, and have it to the
full" (John 10:10, NIV). Yes, you are the apple of His eye. College
is a time to grow, learn, explore and renew your vows with Him.

Challenge: Build your house on a rock and not sand. Know the Bible
by reading and learning. His Word will never return to you void!

Prayer: Thank You for calling me Your child.

Love always,
Grandma, Aunt Lynne and friend

Guilt vs. False Guilt

"As far as the east is from the west,
so far has he removed our transgressions from us."
Psalm 103:12 (NIV)

Guilt is worry that is rooted in fear. Millions of people destroy their lives worrying about something in the past that they are unable to do anything about—the seemingly ever-present cloud of guilt. When God forgives our sin He also removes the guilt. Just as we must receive His forgiveness we must also receive freedom from guilt and not let that emotion control us.

Frequently many feel shame and guilt over something that is not in their control or doing. Many carry false guilt their whole lives. This is of the devil, making you feel responsible for something that happened to you that is not of your doing. Satan uses this to keep you in the past and hold you back from fully running toward God in the now. It is as if you lose hope and hit the wall. Dreams vanish, and one worries about what people will think about them. One's life goes round and round, and *now* is the time to stop and ask God for help. *I cried unto the Lord and He heard me. He lifted me out of the miry clay and made me whole. He gave me a new song!* (Psalm 40:1-3, NASB, paraphrased).

Don't let false guilt smother you. You are special and loved by Jesus, friends and family. The minute you realize your self-punishment, Jesus can cleanse your thoughts and memories and give you forgiveness. This allows you to forgive yourself. He will break the chains that bind you!

Challenge: God has big plans for you. So let go and let God! Seeking help is important also. I remember you in my prayers at all times, and let us be encouraged by each other's faith.

Prayer: God, thank You for forgiving my sin and forgetting it. Help me to model forgiveness to others.

Love always,
Grandma, Aunt Lynne and friend

Promises

[Inspired by Joel Osteen's *I Declare: 31 Promises to Speak over Your Life*]
"The Lord is faithful to all his promises."
Psalm 145:13 (NIV)

"I declare I will experience God's faithfulness. I will not worry. I will not doubt. I will keep my trust in Him, knowing that He will not fail me. I will give birth to every promise God put in my heart, and I will become everything God created me to be!" [4] Remember that what you say is what you are. I read about this several years ago, and it really is true. What you thought about three years ago is what you are becoming.

Just because you don't see anything happening doesn't mean God is not working. Do not give up and become discouraged. Just because it is taking a long time does not mean it is over. Just because your emotions say "no way!" does not mean God will not do what He said. God is faithful. It will happen. God is in complete control, always. More than three thousand promises are recorded in the Bible. It says in Hebrews 13:5-6, "I will never fail you. I will never abandon you. So we can say with confidence, 'The Lord is my helper, so I will have no fear. What can mere people do to me?'" (NLT). God will not fail you. He will not let you down. The problems will not overtake you. It is so good to hear words of affirmation!

Challenge: Dare to trust Him and His promises. God has you in the palm of His hand. This is the good news. This author speaks to my heart—return to the top of the page and repeat it again and again. Let's grow stronger together!

Prayer: May I turn to You for support and confirmation!

Love always,
Grandma, Aunt Lynne and friend

Promises, Again

[Inspired by Joel Osteen's *I Declare: 31 Promises to Speak over Your Life*] [5]
"The tongue has the power of life and death."
Proverbs 18:21 (NIV)

What you say is what you are. This means we will get what we say. If you want to know what you will be three to five years from now, just listen to what you are saying about yourself. Do not speak defeat about your future; instead, speak blessings. Proverbs 6:2 says that we are "snared with the words of [our] mouth" (NASB). Who can control the tongue?

If you get up in the morning feeling the blahs, don't ever say, "This will be a lousy day." No, get up and say, "This is going to be a great day! I am excited about my future because God is with me." That is why on a regular basis we should say, "I am blessed, I'm healthy, I'm strong, I'm valuable, I'm talented, I have a bright future, and I am getting better and better every day!" Remember that you are strong in the Lord!

Challenge: Don't use words to describe the situation; use words to change the situation. Declare, I am blessed; I have the favor of God; He has a plan for my life; I am strong; I am healthy, and I am valuable!

Prayer: I am because You are, God. I need these words of hope every day.

Love always,
Grandma, Aunt Lynne and friend

Manna

"In the morning you will be filled with bread.
Then you will know that I am the Lord your God."
Exodus 16:12 (NIV)

God provided for His own. The Israelites were wandering home-less in the desert for forty years, and each morning God sent them a miracle — manna. The people had instructions to gather only what they needed for the day. No hoarding, for it would go sour. This intended blessing would spoil by their lack of faith when they disobeyed His command to trust for provision beyond today. Jesus does not give tomorrow's manna (blessing) today. We can rely on Jesus' lead for today, stepping out in faith with Him and trusting in tomorrow.

Challenge: "Do not worry for tomorrow; for tomorrow will care for itself" (Matthew 6:34, NASB). He will provide for all of our needs "according to His riches in glory in Christ Jesus" (Philippians 4:19, NASB). "Cease striving and know that I am God." (Psalm 46:10, NASB).

Prayer: God, help me to know You are there for me, and I will step out in faith believing. You truly are my God, the Lord of my life.

Love always,
Grandma, Aunt Lynne and friend

My Prayer

"My soul yearns for you in the night;
in the morning my spirit longs for you."
Isaiah 26:9 (NIV)

I long for You, Lord, as in a dry and dusty land. I thirst for You and need Your presence in my life. Jesus, come to me as if in the night. The shadows stir me, knowing I am restless—I hunger for a word from You.

Leaving my writing for a few days makes me realize I am nothing without You whispering in my ear. I see the days remaining after my rest, and I know You are running after me, and I say, "Thank You." Again You have heard my cry, and I am returned to peace. You are the Master, and I am Your servant.

Love always,
Grandma, Aunt Lynne and friend

Original painting by Lynne Granger

Future Spouse

"But seek first the kingdom of God and His righteousness,
and all these things will be added to you."
Matthew 6:33 (ESV)

*D*ear Lord,
*If it is Your will, I pray that these college kids and gradu-
ates will be united in a loving and Christian marriage. Keep them
sexually pure so they will honor You with their bodies and minds.
As they seek a spouse who will honor and care for them, give them
patience and discernment.*

I have noticed some of you are wearing promise rings for purity.
This is great as it glorifies God. I remember when my husband and
I went to Washington, D.C., at the Washington Memorial, where a
thousand young people where gathered through Youth for Christ. So
many of them knelt with their parents to make this promise: *I will
be pure.* From the distance we saw the whole field filled with young
people raising their hands and glorifying God.

The marriage/divorce ratio today is forty/sixty. Remember: God
is still God, and He has His hand on you. So look up and not down.

Challenge: I will be patient, trust the Lord and give Him all my heart.

Prayer: May my choice for a life partner be Your choice so we may
glorify You in a lasting love.

Love always,
Grandma, Aunt Lynne and friend

Choose Joy

"This is the day that the Lord has made; let us rejoice and be glad in it."
Psalm 118:24 (ESV)

S o many of you are sick with the N1H1 flu, and you are forced to be still. So make the choice to "Be still, and know that I am God" (Psalm 46:10, NKJV). Recall all the Bible verses or lessons you have learned. This will bring peace that will quiet your heart and mind and help you to heal.

God is not a dictator but a loving God who allows you to choose. You can choose joy even if you feel like crap! This is Great-Grandma Granger's word. This kind of joy lifts you up and flows out of you like living water. Joy is a verb, an action word. "This is the day that the Lord has made; let us rejoice and be glad in it" (Psalm 118:24, ESV), verb being *let us rejoice!*

God is near to those who call upon His name, and He can let you live in confidence. This confidence does not depend on outward circumstances, but on the presence of God. This is the time of prayer; I choose petition, praise and thanksgiving (petition being: I choose love; therefore I will love).

God loves you and wants you to grow in His likeness. We are nothing without Him. So do you choose life or separation? He is here to tend to your wounds, your need and, yes, your choices! The key is "I choose."

I have touched the surface, but if you copy this and make it part of your walk you will feel His love and the presence of the Holy Spirit.

Challenge: Do not turn away. Call upon Him for all truth. He chose you, so you choose Him.

Prayer: Thank You, God. When I call on You I can count on You to hear my cry.

Love always,
Grandma, Aunt Lynne and friend

What Should I *Do?*

"Know that the Lord has set apart the godly for himself;
the Lord hears when I call to him."
Psalm 4:3 (ESV)

L et me first clarify that *do* is an action word.
What if your loved one begins to slip away from God or your family? One has a choice: confront like a general, or pull back. Neither of these is the answer!

When prayer is the only option you are in an excellent position to see God move. Remember God loves and cares for you. Pray and believe God's promises: "Call to me and I will answer you and tell you great and unsearchable things you do not know" (Jeremiah 33:3, NIV), and "I will not leave nor forsake you" (Hebrews 13:5, ESV).

Challenge: Quit maneuvering and crying and get serious about calling on God so incredible things will happen. I don't mean to be harsh, but God is a loving God and will move mightily to answer your prayers. The amazing truth is that God cannot resist those who humbly and honestly cry out to Him, those who realize how much they desperately need Him. He will always respond, even if it's not always what we want. He knows what is best because He has the big picture. Remember that, when you are accounted for, it is the intent of the heart that matters. My words are those of a person who has walked through the fire but eventually saw the light and everlasting arms of God; He loves us and is real! Learning the concept—"the intent of the heart"—released me from many chains that had bound me for several years. The reality of this brought tears of joy and relief. That which was hazy became clear like sunshine after a storm. Again, His light released me from darkness.

Prayer: Lord, align my heart and desires to Your will.

Love always,
Grandma, Aunt Lynne and friend

What, Again?

"'For my thoughts are not your thoughts, neither are your ways my ways,'
declares the Lord. 'As the heavens are higher than the earth, so are my
ways higher than your ways and my thoughts than your thoughts.'"
Isaiah 55:8-9 (NIV)

How would you respond if someone told you the gospel is
foolishness or that they cannot be bothered with memorizing
Scripture? Memorizing the gospel is a starting point, a new beginning, in your walk with Christ. We cannot side-step this necessity.

The freshness and immediacy of the Word frees us from sec-
ondhand clichés and stock-in-trade answers. When connecting with
God, He gives us the words of wisdom and knowledge appropriate
for the occasion. The gift of God and His Son, Jesus Christ, is His
presence in the fullness of His kingdom. We must play an important
part in God's whole mission in the world. This is not only for others
but for you too, so that you fulfill your call throughout all your life.
Remember that God does not take vacations! Study in order to know
thoroughly the many nuances of the good news: peace, love, healing,
patience, kindness and so on. We are all to be stewards of the Word.

Challenge: Ask yourself, *how might God use me to spread the good
news both personally and to others?* Whether alone, on campus or
abroad, He is counting on you!

Prayer: God, I give up trying to fit You into my mold. Instead, let
me strive to fit into Your plans. Stop me from trying to organize You!
(The Lord must laugh a lot at what we say about Him).

Love always,
Grandma, Aunt Lynne and friend

God Is an Awesome God

"For God is working in you, giving you the desire
and the power to do what pleases Him."
Philippians 2:13 (NLT)

We sometimes wonder if we are good enough when we should know God is good enough. Two years ago my husband and I went to the Eastern High School reunion. We saw many friends, but one young woman came up to me whom I did not recognize. She started to tell me how I had prayed for her many years ago at a similar function. You see, after that program, she was planning on going home to commit suicide...WOW. But she did not as a result of the care and power of prayer. What would have happened if I had not stepped out in faith and prayed for her? Some would call it stupidity, but not me. This was my challenge, and, yes, I felt clumsy. You see, it is not *who you are*, but *who He is in* our lives.

Challenge: I love God and depend on Him. Won't you, even when you feel clumsy, fearful, inadequate and unsure?

Prayer: God, I ask that You come into my life with Your power, light, life, answers and forgiveness.

Love always,
Grandma, Aunt Lynne and friend

Don't Just Dream Your Dream–Live It

"A man's heart plans his way, but the Lord directs his steps."
Proverbs 16:9 (NKJV)

Few things in life create more worry, stress and fear than the future. The future sometimes seems so mysterious and uncertain. And, oh, how you can fill your mind with all kinds of "what ifs." What if I'm alone forever? What if this pain I'm having is something more serious? And what if none of my dreams comes true? Am I really serving the Lord with my gifts?

Dreams require discipline and faithfulness day after day. Remember the harvest is never in the same season that you plant. "Let us not become weary in doing good, for at the proper time we will reap a harvest if we do not give up" (Galatians 6:9, NIV).

Are you playing it safe by avoiding risks and challenges? You can choose to follow your own path, or you can walk down the road to the life God had for you before you were even born!

Challenge: Are people drawn to you because you radiate the love of God? We should always do our best with what we have no matter what it is. God has a dream for you—a dream that is uniquely yours. He puts the dream in your heart, and then He waits. He waits for you to call out to Him, to pray and seek Him with your whole heart. Are you willing to respond to His dream for you?

Prayer: God, help me to apply this to my life and live my dreams and get rid of negative thoughts and words, and seek You with all my heart.

Love always,
Grandma, Aunt Lynne and friend

His Word

"And the peace of God, which transcends all understanding,
will guard your hearts and your minds in Christ Jesus."
Philippians 4:7 (NIV)

T his is one verse that is already in my back pocket and ready to serve me when I feel uneasy, panicky and anxious. Having migraine headaches and the ensuing pain, I *need* the comfort of memorized Bible verses. When these times come, I breathe deeply of the spiritual oxygen found in these words. His Word becomes life-like. When I was a senior in college, these verses began to speak to and feed my hungry heart. I call verses like this life-line verses. I would feel God's calling and purpose in my life. God speaks profoundly and powerfully through His Word.

Challenge: Set up a folder and build a list of verses that speak to your heart. This referral list is food in time of famine and in time of rejoicing. Before you go to sleep, pick a verse, commit it to memory and integrate it into your life.

Prayer: Father, help students of all ages with the ability to absorb Your Word totally in their lives. Touch each one with Your presence, guidance, love and power.

Love always,
Grandma, Aunt Lynne and friend

New Chapter

"And the prayer offered in faith will make the sick person well;
the Lord will raise them up."
James 5:15 (NIV)

I went to my doctor yesterday, and he said, "Oh, good, it's you." It was obvious he was in a lot of pain. I asked if I could pray for him, and he gratefully replied, "Oh, yes, please!" I prayed, and then, in his pain, he prayed for me. Come to find out, I was the only one who offered up prayer that day. If I had not inquired, we both would have missed the blessing!

I share this because God's Word and presence in James 5:15 can take the form of a cup of coffee, a call or an e-mail. All it takes is to reach out to one another. Such a small token is great in the Lord.

Challenge: As young people and old, at certain times in our lives, we become wounded soldiers, and if we touch one another, even in our brokenness, His presence comes alive through us. We should not separate the physical and the spiritual, as Jesus Christ is Lord over both the body and the soul.

Prayer: God, I know I am not alone. So fill me with Your presence so I can support and pray for others. Help me to be sensitive to all those in need and help me in my brokenness.

Love always,
Grandma, Aunt Lynne and friend

Give God What You Are Not

"He will give you beauty for ashes, joy instead of mourning, praise
instead of despair. For the Lord has planted them like strong and
graceful oaks for his own glory."
Isaiah 61:3 (NLT)

And He will give abundantly, overflowing with great power,
direction and love! *New York Times* best-selling author Joyce
Meyer has taught me through her life that if you give God everything
you are and are not He will give you everything He is, and has, that
is for your benefit. Victory is not about what you can do; it's about
what God can do through you. If you give all those things that are
worn and torn, then He will make something awesome out of them.
Let God begin to flow through your strengths and weaknesses.

Challenge and Prayer: God, take everything I am, and everything
I am not, and use it for Your purpose! In Jesus' name, amen.

Love always,
Grandma, Aunt Lynne and friend

Take Your Messes and Turn Them into Miracles

"Forgetting the past, and looking forward to what lies ahead,
I strain to reach the end of the race and receive the prize."
Philippians 3:13-14 (TLB)

P aul tried fixing earlier mistakes and discovered how complicated it was. It seemed impossible. We can do only one thing with the past: give it to God. When we take our messes and give them to God, He has the ability to turn our mistakes for our greater good, if we trust Him to do so.

Every day is a new day containing tremendous possibilities: new life, new hopes and new dreams. Let go of what's behind and move forward. Get your mind out of the past in order to see God's plan for today. Give up self-pity and discouragement. This is difficult, but this is freedom.

Challenge: Perhaps you need to look up and around instead of back and down. Don't spend your life mourning what you have lost and what is already gone. Take an inventory of what you have left and keep going, one step at a time. This sounds easy but is not. You will find that what you give to God will multiply.

Prayer: God, help me not to dwell on my past. Instead, help me grow in my relationship with You. God, love me like I have never been loved before. I want to turn my life over to You, and please take my messes and turn them into miracles (this is a lifetime prayer of training).

Love always,
Grandma, Aunt Lynne and friend

Faith

"Seek, and you will find; knock, and it will be opened unto you."
Matthew 7:7 (ESV)

G od loves you beyond anything you can conceive of or hope for. It is time to rest in Him, totally without care. It is time, in your spirit, to "be still, and know that [He is] God" (Psalm 46:10, ESV). Stop running and going in circles. You will wear yourself out. "Faith comes by hearing, and hearing by the Word of God" (Romans 10:17, NKJV).

I can promise you that God has a plan for your life, a plan that can change with the seasons of life. I have discovered this for myself as I have gotten older. Remember it is who you are in God's eyes that is most important! God sees you as so special. It's like the saying, *When I count my blessings, I count you twice!*

Challenge: College is tough, but I know you can do it! You have so many resources around you—like counseling—both academic and personal. It is only shameful if you *do not* reach out, and take advantage. This can be an opportunity to stretch and grow you.

Prayer: "I don't mean to say that I have already achieved these things or that I have already reached perfection" (Philippians 3:12, NLT). But with Your help, God, let's work together.

Love always,
Grandma, Aunt Lynne and friend

Put Muscle on Your Faith

"My power works best in weakness. So now I am glad to boast about my
weakness, so that the power of Christ can work through me.
That's why I take pleasure in my weaknesses. . .
For when I am weak, then I am strong."
2 Corinthians 12:9-10 (NLT)

I t is easy to dream if all you have to do is sit on the bench, but you don't make a basket from the bench or win the game from the locker room. You have to get into the court of life. Yes, this takes courage and hard work—study and more study. If you are going to win the tournament, exercise your faith—taking risky steps in the process so your faith will grow.

Dare to trust God; dare to follow God; put muscle on your faith. I will work to put more muscles on my new knee to make it work better. Your dreams force your faith to become stronger and more powerful. If faith is the result of a God-given dream, then the work is worth it!

Challenge: I'm willing to go through the "practices" so I can be a better "player" in life. A musician would say "rehearsals," and an artist would say "sessions."

Prayer: I'm so tired of sitting on the bench, Lord. Especially the right side, when I want to be in the middle with my coach, so I can get into the game faster.

Love always,
Grandma, Aunt Lynne and friend

Expectations and Thank You

"But those who hope in the Lord will renew their strength."
Isaiah 40:31 (NIV)

Thank You for being the light of my heart, my life and those around me.

What are you expecting in life—good things, bad things, big things, little things? Hope: confident expectations. Hope is first. Expectations set the limits of your life. If you never expect good things, or bad things to get better, then they won't. God promises to meet you at your level of expectancy. Have what your faith expects! Start expecting to overcome every challenge you face.

Challenge: Live every day of your life expecting God to bless you abundantly above and beyond your wildest dreams. I will believe this with all my heart, knowing hope will not fail me!

Prayer: This is a hard prayer, but refine me and whittle me down so I can be made for Your glory.

Love always,
Grandma, Aunt Lynne and friend

Don't Panic!

"For in this hope we were saved. But hope that is seen is not hope at all.
Who hopes for what they already have?"
Romans 8:24 (NIV)

God's normal way of operation is not to show His plan for our lives ahead of time. Groaning won't help. God promises to be your sun and your shield. He will carry you with His strong and loving right arm. His love is greater than the morning stars or the moon. You are His child, so we should stop pleading for God to show us the future and start living and obeying like we are confident that He holds the future. Today is the day that counts!

Don't panic. Thank Him for the promises He has for you in His Word. Start looking and claiming these powerful promises that have withstood the test of time. God always loves you and wants the very best for your life.

Challenge: You are a kid of the kingdom—don't forget it. Ask Him to walk with you, for His presence is abundant, and "who can separate us from the love of Christ?" (Romans 8:35, HCSB). He loves you with an everlasting love; you are special.

Prayer: Help me not to be cowering and fearful, but help me behave instead like Your very own child, adopted into Your family, calling You Abba, dear Father. There is no earthly comparison. *We are God's children.*

Love always,
Grandma, Aunt Lynne and friend

Anxiety

"You do not know what tomorrow will bring. What is your life?
For you are a mist that appears for a little time and then vanishes.
Instead you ought to say,
'If the Lords wills, we will live and do this or that.'"
James 4:14-15 (ESV)

Anxiety is simply living out the future before it gets here. We want to know the end from the beginning and that He can be trusted. We want to be in control instead of being content with simple obedience today. Trusting Him should be in our hearts because God is in control, not us. Let us walk by faith and not by sight.

Challenge: Worrying about the future is a sin of unbelief and an indication that our hearts are not resting on the promises of God. Remember to think about others before yourself. Be holy! Love Jesus. These seem like short instructional sentences, but trust me — they are filled with love!

Prayer: God, help me not to worry, but to trust You in all things. I wait patiently to be filled with Your presence so I can move forward.

Love always,
Grandma, Aunt Lynne and friend

I Will Use My Words to Bless People

"Confess your sins to each other and pray for each other
so that you may be healed."
James 5:16 (NLT)

A round you are scores of people hungry to have someone say something nice about them. You could be that person. Does it not make your day? Speak favor and victory over friends and loved ones. Tell them you're proud of them, that they are amazing, talented and beautiful. When you speak blessings over friends, family or acquaintances you are not just saying nice words, but words that carry supernatural power. These words can be a turning point in their lives. Be sure you ask for God's special presence when you bless someone. . .it is so simple, and it can have such a huge impact. That's why you should get in a habit of speaking "the blessing" every chance you get.

Challenge: Make this your mission and make someone's day by reaching out and touching them with kind, loving words.

Prayer: Lord, help me to touch someone so Your presence will flow from me to them, so their needs will be met. I love Your holy touch.

Love always,
Grandma, Aunt Lynne and friend

With God All Things Are Possible

"For nothing is impossible with God."
Luke 1:37 (NLT)

There is nothing too hard with God. There is nothing God cannot do because His power is unlimited. God has absolute power over the storms of life and the storms of nature. He has far more power than is necessary to meet your needs. May He lift you above your present circumstances and help you do things you could not do without Him. If God is so powerful that He can create something from nothing, then think what He can do in your life. He has the power to do whatever is necessary, and He does not want you to doubt it!

Challenge: "Trust in the Lord with all your heart, and lean not on your own understanding; in all your ways acknowledge Him, and He shall direct your paths" (Proverbs 3:5-6, NKJV).

Prayer: God, I acknowledge that nothing is too hard for You—not even changing the most difficult circumstances and decisions of life. Right now I ask that You fill me with the presence of Your Holy Spirit and with Your love, peace and joy. Enable me by the infilling of Your Spirit. I acknowledge right now that my prayers are being answered, whether I feel it or not!

Love always,
Grandma, Aunt Lynne and friend

Do I Have to Be in the Corner Again?

"The steadfast love of the Lord never ceases; his mercies never come
to an end;
they are new every morning; great is your faithfulness."
Lamentations 3:22-23 (ESV)

When a child is put in the corner, for whatever reason, I know how that feels. As an adult, have you ever found yourself in a corner with fear, anxiety, illnesses, pain and loneliness? It seems as if you will be stuck there forever.

As I rested last night, I was reminded that by using the name of Jesus my fears turned to *joy, which is my strength* (Nehemiah 8:10, NIV, paraphrased). Just say *Jesus*. You see, Jesus loves you with an everlasting love, and His presence surrounds you with healing power. We tend to hide our lack of wholeness and are not able to reach out to others—we wear masks, which prevents vulnerability that could otherwise be the door to strong relationships.

I used to sing a rhyme to our four children:

Jesus loves you when you're good; He loves you when you're glad.

Jesus loves you when you're sad; He loves you when you're bad.

Challenge: Let's remember this rhyme, so in turn we can reach out to others in compassion, the way Jesus reaches out to us.

Prayer: Help me, God, to continue to walk in Your unconditional love, even when I have missed the mark. And help me always to be a good friend and neighbor!

Love always,
Grandma, Aunt Lynne and friend

God's Will

"In the day of prosperity be happy, but in the day of adversity consider—
God has made the one as well as the other so that man
will not discover anything that will be after him."
Ecclesiastes 7:14 (NASB)

C oncerning our obsession with finishing God's will, this thought may be most crucial: We have too many choices. Previous generations didn't have as many choices ahead of them. Mother Granger found it difficult to relate to our dilemma because her generation was concerned with the day-by-day living. They felt more of a sense of duty to family, citizenship and church.

Students today have multiple interests and capabilities; they have gobs of talent and opportunities. The choices they are confronted with are mind-boggling. Stop and think—choices. *What are you going to do once you graduate?* is not a question many students are eager to hear, let alone answer.

It is taking people longer to settle down. God's plan can include risk—and an opportunity to show courage. We do not have a promise as to what our future here looks like. We have to take risks for God! Simply do what is right and forge ahead even if you don't have a specific word from God. He speaks to us in Scripture where we can start looking at His character and His promises—and thereby have confidence to take risks for His name.

Because we have confidence in God's will of decree, we can radically commit ourselves to His will of desire, without fretting over a hidden will of direction.

Challenge: Hold fast to the Word of God in difficult circumstances or unpopular situations. To some it means getting off your duff and getting a job, or overcoming your fear of rejection and pursuing a lovely Christian woman or man.

Prayer: God, I'm tired of fighting. Help me to commit myself to Your will without whining.

Love always,
Grandma, Aunt Lynne and friend

We All Count

"But Ruth said, 'Do not urge me to leave you or turn back from following
you; for where you go, I will go, and where you lodge, I will lodge.
Your people shall be my people, and your God, my God.'"
Ruth 1:16 (NASB)

S cripture is a vast tapestry of God's creating, saving and blessing
in the world. Example: As an outsider, Ruth became great-grandmother of David and ancestor of Jesus.

Every last one of us does count, just as an obscure outsider and
immigrant woman, Ruth, played such a key role in God's story. God
does have a plan. Even when we are alone God breaks in, shakes
things up, introduces new options and restores us. You see, Ruth didn't
have a clue she would play a key role in God's story (Ruth 4:16-17).

Challenge: Ask God how is it He can pick you up and reach out to
you, a foreigner to His ways, and place you and your family under
His protective wing for generations to come?

Prayer: Bless my family as they identify talents You have given
them to develop. Help me to be a proud encourager of the gifts You
have given them. May they listen to Your "whisperings" deep within
themselves so their contributions also affect generations to come.

Love always,
Grandma, Aunt Lynne and friend

God's Plans

"'I will be found by you,' declares the Lord, 'and will
bring you back from captivity.'"
Jeremiah 29:14 (NIV)

How encouraging are the Lord's words recorded in the book of Jeremiah. There is a big difference between dreaming dreams and living your dreams. So many people are willing to let God give them dreams, but they never take the next step. They never do what it takes to live their dreams. So stop being negative and learn Scriptures that relate to God's plan for your life. This is your time so make it count!

Challenge: Take the next step in life courageously, calling on God to help you. He is always listening and willing to help and sustain you.

Prayer: Right now in the name of Jesus, help me to pray these words: "I will be found by You, God, and I want to be in Your fold. I know power and life are in Your Word, and I step forward to claim it as truth!"

Love always,
Grandma, Aunt Lynne and friend

Dream Your Dream

"'For I know the plans I have for you,' declares the Lord, 'plans to prosper you and not to harm you, plans to give you hope and a future.'"
Jeremiah 29:11 (NIV)

God chose your future before you were even born. "Then you will call upon me and come and pray to me, and I will listen to you. You will seek Me and find Me when you search for Me with all your heart" (Jeremiah 29:12-13, NASB). God has a dream for you only. He puts this dream in your heart, and then He waits! He waits for you to call out to Him, to pray and seek Him with your whole heart. Who better than Christ can help you develop your dream?

Challenge: Are you ready to answer God's call for your life? Help me to stop, be still and listen. He is waiting.

Prayer: God, help me to seek You with my whole heart and thank You for waiting. I come, I come just as I am. . . .

Love always,
Grandma, Aunt Lynne and friend

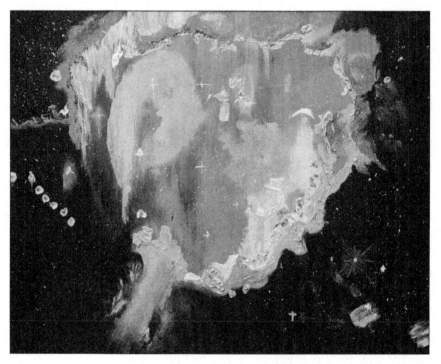

Original painting by Lynne Granger

Be Still and Know I Am God

"Cease striving and know that I am God;
I will be exalted among the nations,
I will be exalted in the earth."
Psalm 46:10 (NASB)

I t's difficult to find a quiet moment. You are constantly on the move. Moments with God don't just happen with a full schedule. Life is scheduling, so why not schedule Him into your life? Something worth doing takes discipline and hard work. This letter is short and sweet, but so very true. Try it!

Challenge: I can and will make an appointment with myself to rest, plan, regroup and draw closer to God to become inwardly balanced.

Prayer: Help me choose to turn the knob and enter into Your presence.

Love always,
Grandma, Aunt Lynne and friend

Be an Overcomer

"I have told you these things, so that in me you may have peace. In this world you will have trouble. But take heart! I have overcome the world."
John 16:33 (NIV)

At age fourteen, I asked Jesus into my heart. I knew something powerful had happened, and my life changed forever. God's plan was not thwarted when family, teachers and friends said I was incapable of obtaining my goals. God had given me meaning and purpose!

God doesn't present obstacles; He presents *the Way*. He became my enabler and provider, and I was finally on my way. Each need and answer brought me closer to God. No way was I going to let Him down and quit. I don't have all the answers, but I have His presence, His counsel, and I learned to lean on Him. His promises are for all, and *if you have not, it is because you ask not* (James 4:2, KJV2000, paraphrased).

God promises to be your rock and your shield. He understands your pain. Cry out for God, and He will protect you with His strong right arm, and your pain will be someone else's gain. God can use you in it. It is important to stay true to your commitment no matter where life finds you.

Challenge: Don't panic. Stand on His promises and be an overcomer.

Prayer: Here I am, God. I'm stopping because this is the day and the hour I have made the decision to trust and follow You.

Love always,
Aunt Lynne, Grandma and friend

My Prayer II

"Taste and see that the Lord is good."
Psalm 34:8 (NLT)

I don't feel well, Lord. I am still; I am trying to still my thoughts on You because You heal the brokenhearted both physically and emotionally.

God, You say You will heal; so come quickly and touch me once again. My bones are weary, and my stomach is tied up in knots.

I am going to take some free time and praise You, even when all things seem gloomy. I seek Your kindness, Your love and forgiveness. Please help me to *be still and know without a doubt that you are God* (Psalm 46:10, ESV, paraphrased). Come quickly, Lord Jesus, as my heart longs for Your presence. Calm my soul, Lord, and slow the beating of my heart. I come; I come.

Love always,
Grandma, Aunt Lynne and friend

Healing

"Pray for each other so that you may be healed."
James 5:16 (NIV)

As the sun peeks over the trees and its purple hue seeks to paint on the pool, so my heart longs for Your eternal touch. It is like going to church knowing Your touch and Your words speak ever so lightly; once again I am whole.

Because You touch me, allow me to touch others with Your healing power. My friend Lydia and I are claiming this Bible verse, that when we pray for one another we will be healed—*if not in this life, then in the next*. She has been a wonderful helpmate, prayer partner and companion as this book began to unfold.

Prayer and Challenge: Pray with your friends, in faith, that you may be healed! And may He be glorified.

Love always,
Grandma, Aunt Lynne and friend

God Hears Us When We Pray

"I love the Lord, for he heard my voice; he heard my cry for mercy.
Because he turned his ear to me, I will call on him as long as I live."
Psalm 116:1-2 (NIV)

D o you have someone in your life who really listens to you?
If so, you are blessed. We all experience times of hurt and seemingly feel alone. Remember, as a child of God, He alone will *always* listen to you. "I waited patiently for the Lord; he turned to me and heard my cry" (Psalm 40:1, NIV), and He made me whole. God is never so far away that He cannot hear us. He loves us and is ever present in our lives.

Challenge: Call to Him. He alone has the power to change your situation. Take comfort in the reality that God loves you.

Prayer: I really cry to You, God. For as long as I live, I will call on You.

Love always,
Grandma, Aunt Lynne and friend

Contentment

"I have learned the secret of being content in any and every situation,
whether well fed or hungry, whether living in plenty or in want."
Philippians 4:12 (NIV)

When asking my niece Lydia how she was doing, she answered, "I have learned to be content!" This was amazing because her family was out of the country and she was staying with her grandparents, still going to school. (Do not misunderstand—grandparents are important.)

Paul knew how to be content whether he had much or little. The secret was Christ's power in His life. Do you have great needs, or are you discontent because you don't have what you *want*? Learn to rely on God's promises—Jeremiah 29:11, Romans 8:18—and Christ's power to help you be content. Ask God to teach you contentment in every situation.

Philippians 4:13 says, "For I can do everything through Christ, who gives me strength" (NLT). Commitment is habitual—a decision—and when joined with God shines with a strong light. Commitment is a fixed temperament of the soul which is not casual, but constant.

Challenge: You must trust God that you will and do know enough to be the person God wants you to be and live the life God wants you to live. This is the cultivation of something positive from your Christ-centered roots. . .so way to go, Lydia!

Prayer: Help me, God, to be content when things do not go the way I think they should.

Love always,
Grandma, Aunt Lynne and friend

Stewards of Prayer

"In the same way, the Spirit helps us in our weakness. We do not know what we ought to pray for, but the Spirit himself intercedes for us with groans that words cannot express...the Spirit intercedes for the saints in accordance to God's will."
Romans 8:26-27 (NIV)

As stewards and saints, we have both the privilege and responsibility to pray for others and for ourselves. To pray is our duty — do not give up. Patience and hope help us in prayer. The greatest helper is the Holy Spirit who helps us in our weakness; He adds His wisdom to our experience. He pleads for us and in us so we can pray mightily in agreement with the will of God. There is so much power in the Holy Spirit.

Challenge: When was the last time you were prompted by the Holy Spirit to pray for a person or situation? Try writing a letter to God using an outline with at least two sentences of the following categories:

(ACTS):

Adoration
Confession
Thanksgiving
Supplication

Prayer: Thank You for the Holy Spirit who intercedes on my behalf to You.

Love always,
Grandma, Aunt Lynne and friend

Family Reunion

"I was glad when they said to me, 'Let us go to the house of the Lord.'"
Psalm 122:1 (ESV)

I look around this special Sunday, August 3, 2014, as our family joins together for a family reunion in Leland. My husband and I have been married fifty-two years, and we are blessed. Many of our children and grandchildren are providing music this morning while the rest of us are attentive to His presence.

Challenge: When we make a commitment, God honors it and helps us grow to be the kind of person and family He wants us to be—it is always for our good and for His glory.

Prayer: Lord Jesus, fill us to overflowing so we can once again spread Your touch. I am so grateful for Your touch at fourteen and how those seeds of life multiply and grow.

Love always,
Grandma, Aunt Lynne and friend

Seeds

"And my God will meet all your needs according
to the riches of His glory in Christ Jesus."
Philippians 4:19 (NIV)

If you have a heart to sow He will provide the seed. Are you willing to seek and find what is inside you that needs cultivating and watering? God will nurture and provide.

"Meanwhile we groan, longing to be clothed instead with our heavenly dwelling" (2 Corinthians 5:2, NIV). God loves you with an everlasting love and will carry you to that place He has set before you—a place where the sun shines and rest abides.

If we come before Him, He will anoint us with the Holy Spirit. Today we can be joyful and celebrate because our seed has taken root. We will be nurtured if we allow Him to work in us. His Son will shine on us, and we will be blessed knowing God is touching us.

Challenge: Let your heart sow the seeds He has provided.

Prayer: I continually come to You, God, and bring my seed before You. Shine on it, and I will be blessed because when harvest time comes I will bear fruit.

Love always,
Grandma, Aunt Lynne and friend

Good Morning, Lord

"I led them with cords of human kindness, with ties of love. To them I
was like one who lifts a little child to the cheek,
and I bent down to feed them."
Hosea 11:4 (NIV)

*Fear not, for I am with you, each step of the way. I have come
to serve you, and you have come to serve Me. I am the God
of Abraham and Isaac, and I am your God. Come and be filled with
My presence and the Holy Spirit. I shall anoint you, and your path
shall be made straight. I shall take your infirmities and use them for
My glory. Because you have been faithful, I shall make your paths
straight. Because you have come before Me seeking My will, I shall
give you abundantly My vision, hope and healing. Continue to follow
Me, and I shall restore you.*

Challenge: I *do* love You, Lord, and I *do* lift my voice to worship
You, O my Lord and King. I come; yes, I come, to serve You.

Prayer: I am blessed, Lord, as I seek Your face. You alone are my
God. I come to be filled with Your presence (this is true praise).

Love always,
Grandma, Aunt Lynne and friend

Call Out

"Your Father knows what you need before you ask Him."
Matthew 6:8 (NIV)

*G*od, *I need You*. The pagans repeat the names of their gods or the same words over and over without thinking. It is important when making a refuge to have a calm and quiet soul, and what is more fitting than to use the phrase from Psalm 136, "Give thanks to the Lord," repeatedly?

Challenge: Persistent prayer is good, but God condemns the shallow repetition of words that are not offered with a sincere heart.

Prayer: God, I know You are here, and I call upon Your name, for You are worthy. Needing You is a longing of my spirit, Your Holy Spirit. Come and renew my heart and life. Again, *I need You!*

Love always,
Grandma, Aunt Lynne and friend

We Are Called Children of God

"See what great love the Father has lavished on us, that we should be
called children of God! And that is what we are!"
1 John 3:1 (NIV)

A gain I arise to greet the morning. May I follow You, O Lord. The colors of the earth shout out to me and tell me You care. I will be anxious for nothing because You are my rock and my shield.

My spirit longs to be filled, and I will not be denied. "You, God, are my God; earnestly I seek you; I thirst for you, my whole being longs for you, in a dry and parched land where there is no water" (Psalm 63:1, NIV). Let me not wander far from Your commandments. My prayer is to be seeking Your delight. Hear my prayer as I call Your name. Together we will walk in love.

The water falls from one rock to quench another. My thirst and my cup runneth over. In seeking Your face, I am satisfied; and again, I am here to greet the morning.

Challenge: I seek Your delight.

Prayer: I thank You, God, for the green pastures where I can come to rest.

Love always,
Grandma, Aunt Lynne and friend

With His Help

"The steps of a man are established by the Lord,
and He delights in his way."
Psalm 37:23 (NASB)

Today I am going to have good thoughts—reminding myself I am a child of God. Today I am going to rest in the Father so that my healing may increase. Today I am going to walk in His steps so I can claim His presence. Because Christ gives life abundantly, I come to be filled. God claims me as His own when I say yes to His calling. Each step and each breath drive me closer to the light and path He has called me to follow.

Challenge: If you would like God to direct your path, then seek His advice before you step out.

Prayer: Jesus, I come because You are real and alive! Each step on campus helps me realize I am where I should be. Let me not veer from Your path and be distracted. Help me to be kind to others and myself.

Love always,
Grandma, Aunt Lynne and friend

The Deer Pants after the Water

"As the deer pants for streams of water,
so my soul pants for you, my God."
Psalm 42:1 (NIV)

Jesus, I am Yours, and I come. Lift me from this drowsy sleep and let me arise to Your truth. I love You, God, knowing You will not be denied. Each word draws me closer to You knowing how inadequate I am. You alone are my source of strength and my guide. Please put a hedge around my loved ones and me, bringing protection and rest. Again my cup runneth over, reassuring me that, yes, I am special in Your sight!

Challenge: Help me to let go of the past; surround me with newness of life. As the deer pants for the water, so my heart longs after You, O Lord.

Prayer: I come, I come. . .I commit.

Love always,
Grandma, Aunt Lynne and friend

Rest for the Weary

"In repentance and rest is your salvation,
in quietness and trust is your strength."
Isaiah 30:15 (NIV)

I lay me down, Lord. Still the beating of my heart. "Come to me, all you who are weary and burdened, and I will give you rest. Take my yoke upon you and learn from me, for I am gentle and humble in heart, and you will find rest for your souls" (Matthew 11:28-29, NIV). You alone, God, are my source of strength, and I beg for mercy — Your ways shall be my ways. Sometimes it is so hard, but I come to You now to lighten my load. Speak to me for I long to hear Your voice and feel Your presence. Cleanse me and make me whole.

As a child, my parents told me the very hairs on my head are numbered and known by You. I will not be afraid, for *I am worth more than many sparrows* (Luke 12:7, NIV, paraphrased). I will take up the cross and follow You, and then I will find life.

Challenge: Help me remember You are gentle and humble at heart. Help me remember Your ability to help me, rather than my inability to help myself.

Prayer: *Why am I discouraged? Why so sad? I will put my hope in God! I will praise Him again—my Savior and my God!* (Psalm 42:5-6, NLT, paraphrased).

Love always,
Grandma, Aunt Lynne and friend

Shining Is Your Witness

[Inspired by T. D. Jakes's *Instinct*] [6]
"I press on toward the goal to win the prize for which
God has called me heavenward in Christ Jesus."
Philippians 3:14 (NIV)

Being in college is demanding and difficult; but you have an inner ability to overcome. God has a vision so you can live a fulfilled life.

Sometimes our talents are like this, peeling off one layer at a time. Focus and stay close to the Lord within you. Don't waste your time being something God did not plant deep inside you. He will let you shine and be more comfortable because you are including Him in your life. As T. D. Jakes says, God has given you *instincts*: a vision which overflows, an inner drive which should be unleashed to free you into the next dimension. God is deep inside you propelling you to the next opportunity. God will not let you be denied, for when you shine He shines.

Challenge: Take time to think, pray and allow God's DNA to *erupt* inside you to be the kind of person He is calling you to be.

Prayer: Show me, God, how my inner gut, my instincts, can *help me to become.* "Wise words are like deep waters; wisdom flows from the wise like a bubbling brook" (Proverbs 18:4, NLT).

Love always,
Grandma, Aunt Lynne and friend

Unlock the Treasure within You

"I praise you because I am fearfully and wonderfully made; your works
are wonderful, I know that full well."
Psalm 139:14 (NIV)

Sometimes we need to look back and focus on the inner child.
The need to slow down, take inventory and nurture this inner
child is something that never truly leaves. Have you neglected the
signs along the way, which predispose evidence of who you are
meant to be? What was it as a child that stood out, that nurtured you?
What was the voice within you that said, "I want to be a _____
when I grow up?"

Do you know this is a continual process? When you are thirty,
fifty and seventy-plus, you will still be asking the same question
because He will continue to fill you with creative life.

God can unleash the treasure within you, and He says you are
not a mistake. He cares and has given you this to let you know this
is where you should be.

Challenge: As long as you are listening to the Father, loving His
people and sharing His Word, you are following His will for your life.

Prayer: Slow me down, Lord. Slow the beating of my heart so that
I can *be still, and know that you are God* (Psalm 46:10, ESV, paraphrased), the God of my very being, and that Your whisperings are
ever still deep inside me, waiting to be released like Living Waters.

Love always,
Grandma, Aunt Lynne and friend

Walk in Faith

"When you pass through the waters, I will be with you; and when you
pass through the rivers, they will not sweep over you."
Isaiah 43:2 (NIV)

I t took a lot of faith for Moses to lead the Israelites out of Egypt,
and it took an equal amount of faith for the Israelites to follow
God as they stepped out in faith and put their footprints on the floor
of the Red Sea; they left a lesson for us to follow: *Walk in faith,
believing the God of miracles will not let you down.* "Faith. . .is not
from yourselves; it is the gift of God" (Ephesians 2:8, NIV).

Commit your way to God, and He will keep you from harm. Even
when you stumble, He will catch you and keep you from falling. If
you have been deeply wounded, God will heal you and use your
wounds for His purposes.

Now is the time to step out in faith and make wise choices,
and believe!

Challenge: Believe the God of miracles will not let you down.

Prayer: I commit my way to God. Here I am, Lord. Use me.

Love always,
Grandma, Aunt Lynne and friend

Original painting by Lynne Granger

Dreams

> "And afterward, I will pour out my Spirit on all people. Your sons
> and daughters will prophesy, your old men will dream dreams,
> your young men will see visions."
> Joel 2:28 (NIV)

Future aspirations and hopes are something that will make a difference. We need enough time for things that are important—priorities—choices—spend time off work. It requires discipline and commitment. To me, as an artist, dreams are visual. It is mystical, magical and marvelous.

Life without dreams and visions is not life at all. Christ requires prayer, reading and studying that which God has set before you. Otherwise, we become stale and useless.

Most people stop themselves from reaching their potential. People who achieve their dreams and visions don't have an easier path than those who do not. We should not make excuses; instead look at your attitude. It is your mind-set, your tenacity, that is important in the pursuit of your dreams. The only guarantee for failure is to stop trying! Never, never give up. It's not too late to start again. We have an obligation; *to whom much is given, much is required* (Luke 12:48, ESV, paraphrased).

Key people in my life said, "You can't make it. You don't have what it takes to go to college, find a job or marry Jerry!" That is when I put my shoulders back and said, "I *can*," and with God's help I did!

> *He provided all my needs according to His riches in heaven through Jesus Christ our Lord* (Philippians 4:19, NIV, paraphrased).

Challenge: Dare to dream big!

Prayer: Help me, God, not to make excuses, but to look to You for wisdom and direction.

Love always,
Grandma, Aunt Lynne and friend

I Have Good News for You

"May the God of hope fill you with all joy
and peace as you trust in him."
Romans 15:13 (NIV)

D o you feel fretful, lost and confused? If so, I have good news. He is our power, our strength, because God gives us a sound mind. Believe this, and you will experience Christ's character, mind and presence. The Lord is always before us because He is at my right hand and I will not be shaken. I am not afraid of tomorrow *because I know God is already there*.

Therefore, my heart is glad, and I will rejoice in Galatians and Ephesians and the fruit of the Spirit. This is another opportunity to memorize God's Word, which is food during good and bad times — another way to be blessed.

God is on our side, which allows us to stand tall and be one with Him. He is the deliverer of good news.

Challenge: Be overflowed with hope as you daily walk with the anointing of the Holy Spirit.

Prayer: In the morning and during the day and in all kinds of situations may I have the infilling of the Holy Spirit. I do come to serve the Almighty.

Love always,
Grandma, Aunt Lynne and friend

Once Again

"Blessed are those. . .who walk in the light of your presence."
Psalm 89:15 (NIV)

O nce again You have touched me, and I am glad. Lord, You top the page of my list, and Your name is written in red. I bow my knees before You now and forever because You are the One who has always been there to guide my life. I still seek Your way and Your presence.

Lord, teach me to number my days so I can discover what is most important to You and continue the work I should be doing. Help me to communicate the gospel but also to

Live it out
Mold it and
Balance truth with love.

Challenge: Allow me to represent Christ in all I do and say. I can only do this when You touch me with Your Holy Spirit, Your presence.

Prayer: My prayer is, "The Lord keeps watch over you as you come and go, both now and forever" (Psalm 121:8, NLT).

Love always,
Grandma, Aunt Lynne and friend

Put God First

"Trust in the Lord with all your heart."
Proverbs 3:5 (NIV)

P ut trust in God first. If we put total trust in people they will let us down. We will become suspicious and bitter and lose hope. I have seen this happen, and it is not pretty! Jesus put "hope" in God first. Let us also do this, as no person can ever be absolutely perfect and right. Never trust anything in yourself or anyone else, except by the grace of God.

In Hebrews 10:9, Christ said, "Here I am. I have come to do your will" (NIV).

The purpose of our spiritual training is to get us in the right relationship with Jesus so we can make a covenant with the needs and will of God. So then we are empowered to accomplish His needs. If we make a commitment, let us be transformed by the indwelling of the Holy Spirit and keep that commitment. Never forget this.

Our lives, both as a "student" and a "student of life," become transformed when we put our life and hands in His. In age we grow; in age we mature. Let us find joy and peace in Jesus Christ. Set your path, draw a line in the sand and follow Him always.

Challenge: Get in the right relationship with God.

Prayer: *I trust in you, God, that you will meet all my needs according to your riches in glory* (Philippians 4:19, NIV, paraphrased).

Love always,
Grandma, Aunt Lynne and friend

Portion

[Inspired by T. D. Jakes's *Instinct*]
"Taste and see that the Lord is good; blessed is the one
who takes refuge in him."
Psalm 34:8 (NIV)

P salm 34:8 calls us to "taste and see that the Lord is good" (NIV). God lays a banquet before us; yet often we stand at the table, staring and clinging to the rubbish in our hands. God desires that we feast on knowing and loving Him. We can if we look within and find true satisfaction in Him as our portion.

In his book *Instinct* T. D. Jakes remarks, from this portion you can find a well springing up from your core which is called instinct, your inner drive. This not only helps you survive, but thrive. [7]

Are you restless and unsatisfied, wondering why fulfillment eludes you? Are you uncertain and fearful? There is an urgent message whispering within—we are intrigued by its insistence but afraid to act on its information. Start listening to your own instinct and stop pleasing others. Know what you are born to do by living in sync with your internal rhythm.

It's time to align your actions with your instincts, the inner eardrum of *who you are* and *what* you are meant to do. Reward what is within you and stop beating yourself up. It's the sense of finding your place in life's puzzle (each piece is the sum of the total). You alone have a gift you can contribute to the world, so relax and enjoy the ride.

Grace is sufficient for all your needs. Time isn't lost; it only contributes to the whole.

Challenge: Let go of the rubbish in your hands, so you can feast with the Lord.

Prayer: Help me to hear Your whisper.

Love always,
Grandma, Aunt Lynne and friend

Knowing His Hand

"And your ears shall hear a word behind you, saying,
'This is the way, walk in it,' when you turn to the right
or when you turn to the left."
Isaiah 30:21 (ESV)

After going to bed at 8:00 p.m, I was up at 3:30 a.m. So what do you do at that time in the morning? I decided to start praying. That did not go very well, so I started quoting Bible verses. Once I started, it was amazing how God's Word propelled itself. I prayed again, and the infilling of the Holy Spirit came over me, and I knew Jesus was through and around me. Then I finally could relax knowing I was praying correctly. I was blessed, and joy touched my inner being. I realized I could ask for wisdom as in the book of James.

Challenge: Read the first chapter of James and ask God to give you wisdom about your current circumstances.

Prayer: You say we can ask, and I am asking, Lord.

Love always,
Grandma, Aunt Lynne and friend

Welcome to God's World!

"I chose you and appointed you so that you might go and bear fruit."
John 15:16 (NIV)

I will strengthen and help you. I have chosen you to be my servant, not my slave. I have taken you from the ends and corners of the earth, and called you by name.

God does not call you to wither away, but to flourish and produce good fruit. If God says He will help you, He will!

Challenge: Learn God's Word and seek His spiritual gifts as found in Galatians 5—faith, hope, joy, love, peace, patience, kindness and self-control.

Prayer: God, I believe Your promise to help me so I can produce good fruit.

Love always,
Grandma, Aunt Lynne and friend

The More Factor

"Now to each one the manifestation of the Spirit is
given for the common good."
1 Corinthians 12:7 (NIV)

D o you have a yearning for MORE in your Spirit? Do you lack power, presence, persistence and peace?

It is not always what we do, but what He has done for us. I am talking about the Holy Spirit.

Jesus said that *when I go to the Father, I will leave you a comforter*, which is the Holy Spirit (John 16:7, KJV, paraphrased).

Remove the dark shadow of doubt and simply ask for MORE of the Holy Spirit in your life. Let Him have His way with you and claim God's gifts and direction for your life! (1 Corinthians 12, 13, 14, 15; Ephesians 5). Study, study, study.

When I was presented with this opportunity, I said, "How do you know you have received the Holy Spirit?" It is not always what you feel; it is an act of faith, taking one step at a time. Literally! My first realization was that I now had the ability to pray according to His will. I started praying....

Challenge: This is not a complex matter! *Ask and you will receive* (Matthew 7:7-8, NIV, paraphrased). We are His servants, and we should ask for the More Factor, the Holy Spirit. All you have to say is, *Yes, I come! Yes, I receive!* And you will! This is your fuel, your power. Yes, there is always more! If you don't ask, you won't receive.

Prayer: I do ask for the Comforter who knows my heart and is ready and waiting. So come.

Love always,
Grandma, Aunt Lynne and friend

There Is Power in the Word

"Thy word have I hid in mine heart, that I might not sin against thee."
Psalm 119:11 (KJV)

Hi, everybody. I have come to you with some powerful stuff. It is not complex; it is simple!

God is looking for hearts that will stop for a moment. David said, "I have hidden your word in my heart" (Psalm 119:11, NIV). That means memorizing His words for those days when you feel low, so they will feed your soul when you need them the most. His words are food and nourishment and will feed your spiritual hunger.

Take time and imagine Jesus is putting His everlasting loving arms around you. Now think of some Bible verses—*Jesus loves me!*— again and again. There is power in the Word.

Now pray, listen and invite Christ into your everyday life—that means everything. Find yourself quieting down. Now the thing is to make this a habit so it becomes a reflex.

God will honor this with peace, quiet, wisdom and answers to your complexities. He loves you so much, and He wants you as His beloved child. So come bathe in His presence.

Challenge: Invite Christ into your everyday life.

Prayer: Jesus, come into my heart, forgive my sins, lead me where You want me to go, and thank You for the gift of heaven.

Love always,
Grandma, Aunt Lynne and friend

My Prayer III

"This is the day that the Lord has made;
let us rejoice and be glad in it."
Psalm 118:24 (NIV)

E vening has come, and I haven't spent enough time with You, O God. What did I do that was so important? I rested, and now I thank You for Your healing presence and power.

Loving You is easy because You are so real; I thank You. Your everlasting love comforts me and makes me whole. Thank You for reminding me I am special! Stay with me through the night and speak to my heart. Remind me of the Scriptures You have planted in my heart.

Good night, Lord—I am Yours.

Love always,
Grandma, Aunt Lynne and friend

Serve with a Generous Spirit

"The greatest among you shall be your servant."
Matthew 23:11 (ESV)

For a minute we are going to think about great heroes who have come before us like Moses, Noah, Rebecca, David and Jesse. These people have run the race faithfully. They pioneered with great faith and are now cheering and encouraging us in the stands of glory. From the coliseum to heaven.

Noah demonstrates that one person can make a difference. He spared the world of mankind, which has affected generations, even our family.

Rebecca served others with a generous spirit. She did not put up a fuss when asked to serve. She is known as the bride of Isaac. She not only gave a cup of water, but she also offered two hundred gallons of water to ten camels. One trip to the trough was five gallons, which took three hours. She did not say, "I don't do windows!"

Jesse's son David served with limitations, but one can serve with God's potential. When faced with Goliath, who had been plaguing Saul's kingdom, David did not say *no* to Saul, who had inquired of strong men and his armies to defeat Goliath. But David said, "I can take the land." Here he was, 145 pounds to Goliath's 245 pounds. The odds seemed against him. Saul even offered his armor. Don't let limitations hold you back. "If God be for us who can be against us?" (Romans 8:31, KJV).

Be encouraged. Run the race that is before you. Be strong. Listen to God. He will encourage you. May God bless you.

Challenge: Serve with a generous spirit. Maybe this letter can be shared with your family and friends so they can serve with gratitude.

Prayer: God, I'm listening. Please encourage me and help me serve boldly where I am needed. Let's go!

Love always,
Grandma, Aunt Lynne and friend

Laugh Heartily

"The Lord is my strength and my shield; my heart trusts in him, and he
helps me. My heart leaps for joy, and with my song I praise him."
Psalm 28:7 (NIV)

Have you laughed today?
Have you cried or been depressed today?

Whatever it is, it doesn't matter. In God's eyes He loves you just the way you are and the place where you are.

Some of you are far from home and from God, and you need Him now. He is here for you. All you need to do is say, "Come into my heart, my life. I need You." He has a perfect plan for your life. No one is too far from God. He loves you, and He will never forsake you.

Because He loves, you may also live. Have you stopped to let His everlasting arms enfold you to let you know your value, His pleasure? When you seek Him, you are His pleasure, His favor. You are special. You can become all He has for you.

I come from a very bad physical and emotional background, and I know what it is like to fight through to be a survivor. If I can, by asking Christ into my heart and asking Him to forgive my sins at age fourteen, you can too!

Christ has thousands of promises for you in the Bible. Now is the time to search the Bible for all He has for you.

Now seek Him with all your heart, and you will not be disappointed. He has a plan for your life. God loves all of you! He sees the good in you, a ray of potential. You are His child!

Challenge: Now go in peace believing in His love and humbly serve Him.

Prayer: It's morn, Lord, and I'm claiming Your promise that joy will come!

Love always,
Grandma, Aunt Lynne and friend

Bloom Where You Are Planted

"The steps of a good man are ordered by the Lord."
Psalm 37:23 (KJV)

Today's Scripture verse means that as long as we are in faith and where we are supposed to be, then we can bloom where we are planted.

If we keep the right attitude, God will always use it for good, and we can enjoy the ride!

God is in complete control, and we are part of His divine plan. I have to keep pinching myself and not let myself or anyone else steal my joy. No ifs or buts.

Believe that God has planted you in a certain place so you can help someone else. Let your light shine and make a difference where you are now.

Challenge: My challenge to you is to "be content whatever the circumstances" (Philippians 4:11, NIV). We do not have to like it, but if this helps one person to become who God has created them to be, then I come.

Prayer: Guide my steps, God, and help me to bloom where I am planted.

Love always,
Grandma, Aunt Lynne and friend

The Big "If"

"We know that all things work together for the good of those who love God: those who are called according to His purpose."
Romans 8:28 (HCSB)

I tend to be an "if person," as I often struggle with migraine headaches. I have to work hard at rising above to the joy God has waiting for me.

Some of the "ifs" in life we ask ourselves are, *What if I could*:

Find the perfect job
Meet new friends
Have a better apartment
Have the right roommate
Find God in all of this

The "ifs" kind of thinking will only hold you back from happiness. A better approach is, *This is where God has placed me right now, and until He moves me I will be happy where I am planted!*

Challenge: Let's contemplate what God has for you in this season. Believe He has put you here for a reason. Only God can change the inner you. Knowing this is good; now let us believe in God's presence and experience deep peace, comfort, calmness and joy. Be faithful where you are, and God will nourish and fertilize you for healthy growth.

Prayer: Help me trust You, God, when things are not so easy and to know You are active and at work in my life, in the powerful name of Jesus! I will trust You, God, one step at a time.

Love always,
Grandma, Aunt Lynne and friend

A Father and His Son

"Did not your father have food and drink? He did what was right
and just, so all went well with him."
Jeremiah 22:13-15 (NIV)

L ooking at Jeremiah 22:13-17, I would like to compare a father, Josiah, and his son Jehoiakim and what can happen between two generations when one follows the Lord and one does not.

Josiah was one of Judah's great and faithful kings who taught his son about God by modeling righteous living. He was a fair and just king and reigned many years.

Jehoiakim reigned only three months and was sent to Egypt because he was in everything the opposite of his father. He could not even claim his father's blessings because he did not follow his father's God.

You see, we may inherit our father's possessions, but we cannot inherit their faith or blessings. Some of you have a great inheritance, a good education, and come from a beautiful home. This does not guarantee a strong character. We must choose our own relationship with God. You may not have had a Paul-like conversion, but you can stand or sit where you are and say "I choose Christ". . .and that is what it is all about!

Be a good son or daughter or grandchild, but be cautious and do not lose your focus. Ask yourself, Am I being sucked up by abundance and being comfortable, or am I striving to be more Christ-like? Love God. I care for Him by studying and praying.

I love you so much, and I care for you by studying and praying.

Challenge: Choose your own relationship with God.

Prayer: God, I come and choose You as the focus and meaning in my life.

Love always (as usual),
Grandma, Aunt Lynne and friend

Communication

"All you need to say is simply 'Yes' or 'No'; anything
beyond this comes from the evil one."
Matthew 5:27 (NIV)

R elationships depend on open communication and meaningful
dialogues. This is meant to be an exchange of ideas—one
person speaking while the other listens, and back and forth.

I guess this has come to mind because I have been home and in
bed for four weeks with the flu, which has been an epidemic in our
society. If you have had a similar experience, we too send our love
and prayers.

Communication is a God-given tool to be used to establish and
enjoy relationships. Learn sensible ways to communicate that do
not over stress you but strengthen your relationships. Cultivate your
conversation manners, and you'll reap the rewards of meaningful
human connection.

Challenge: This is the time in life when we should care for each
other and sincerely communicate with each other. It is well worth
the effort. Some of you should not hold back but reach out because
you are really loved. God will give you courage when you need it.
Dare to trust Him for it!

Prayer: "I pray that out of His glorious riches, He may strengthen
you with power through his Spirit in your inner being" (Ephesians
3:16, NIV).

Love always,
Grandma, Aunt Lynne and friend

Bearing Each Other's Burdens

"Two people are better off than one, for they can help each other succeed.
If one person falls, the other can reach out and help.
But someone who falls alone is in real trouble."
Ecclesiastes 4:9-10 (NLT)

S ome days we are not up to par. We often tend to hide how we are feeling. We think we always have to be a hundred percent. "Hey, I am great. I am perfect!" Even Jesus had His "off" days and had to go to the other side of the lake or to the garden where He bled tears of blood while seeking God's will. What is your thorn right now that needs our prayers?

James 5:13-16 says, "Is anyone among you in trouble? Let them pray. Is anyone happy? Let them sing songs of praise. Is anyone among you sick? Let them call the elders of the church to pray over them and anoint them with oil in the name of the Lord. And the prayer offered in faith will make the sick person well; the Lord will raise them up. If they have sinned, they will be forgiven. Therefore confess your sins to each other and pray for each other so that you may be healed" (NIV). Mark this in your Bible, and it will be a reference your whole life long, like a life raft. We are to care for one another.

Even though you ask for our prayers, we can still be your prayer warrior and are even more reminded to pray for you. Remember to bear your thorn in the flesh with someone you can trust, and whom can you trust more than Jesus? He said, "For where two or three gather in my name, there am I with them" (Matthew 18:20, NIV).

Challenge: Stand with someone today and pray for their burdens. If you are going through something challenging, have the boldness to call on a friend and ask for prayer.

Prayer: Lord Jesus, open my eyes to my brothers and sisters around me who need prayer. Help me to be sensitive to the things they are facing, and give me wisdom in how to pray for them.

Love always,
Grandma, Aunt Lynne and friend

Best-Laid Plans

"Why, you do not even know what will happen tomorrow. What is
your life?
You are a mist that appears for a little while and then vanishes. Instead,
you ought to say, 'If it is the Lord's will, we will live and do this or that.'"
James 4:14-15 (NIV)

P lans—we write them. God writes them!

Our best-laid plans run into unforeseen challenges and obstacles from time to time. Even with the finest minds, mistakes can be made. We, like children, cannot demand our own way. It could lead to destruction.

Wouldn't it feel great knowing we are in good hands, feeling the wind blow through our hair and enjoying the ride? God loves it when we write our plans *prayerfully,* allowing Him to bless what He has in store for you. *God is good and will supply all your needs according to His riches in heaven through Jesus our Lord* (Philippians 4:19, NASB, paraphrased).

Challenge: Write out your plans on a sheet of paper. Sit with the Lord for a moment, quiet your heart and ask God what His plans are for your life today.

Prayer: God, I submit my plans to You today and ask for You to guide me down the best path for my life.

Love always,
Grandma, Aunt Lynne and friend

Instinct

[Inspired by T. D. Jakes's *Instinct*]
"Each has his own gift from God."
1 Corinthians 7:7 (ESV)

Following your call can make the critical distinction between what we are good at (our vocation or skill set) and what we were *made for*. God wants you to be engaged with your life's calling. As T. D. Jakes says, our instincts can provide the key to unlocking our most satisfying, productive, joyful lives. [8]

Being human does not exclude us from having instincts and, yes, DNA. Rely on your inner whispering, not what others expect of you. Caution is important.

When we combine God, our inner instincts, DNA and intellect we can pursue our passions, and we will discover fulfillment. Then our strengths will increase, and our talents will make a unique contribution to the world. We will find the people, places and events in life we were created to impact.

Perhaps our answer will not be the voice of God shouting at us from the heavens, but in the whisper of our God-given instincts deep within. This is not a new concept, but one known throughout the ages. The question is, Are you willing to seek deep within you and allow the living waters to rise up like bubbling streams as gifts, so the world can know you are a follower of God, the creator of all?

Challenge: What do you see as your calling?

Prayer: I long for Your whisper, Lord.

Love always,
Grandma, Aunt Lynne and friend

Thanksgiving

"Give thanks to the Lord, for he is good; his love endures forever."
Psalm 118:29 (NIV)

The two words that are the most powerful, life-changing words we could ever say are "Thank you!" First Thessalonians 5:18 says, "Give thanks in all circumstances; for this is God's will for you in Christ Jesus" (NIV).

I know this sounds simple, but so many people miss it. We think we'll be happy when our circumstances change, when we get better classes, dorms or roommates. But the truth is, the key to living a life filled with joy and purpose is to have a grateful attitude in all of your life.

Regardless of the things we are facing today, all of us can find a reason to have gratitude.

Once a year we gather with our families for Thanksgiving, one of the most cherished holidays. When you take the time to celebrate the things you are grateful for, a spirit of thanksgiving fills your heart and ministers to every area of your life. When this happens it becomes impossible for you to be discouraged. I am suggesting we have this attitude every day, not just on Thanksgiving.

Start today! You can turn around a troubled relationship, heal a family or restore a friendship. Stop complaining and choose to be positive, and don't take life for granted. You are not ordinary because God loves you as His pride and joy.

Challenge: Gratitude can change your life. What are you thankful for today?

Prayer: I love You, Lord, and I'm trying not to take my life for granted.

Love always,
Grandma, Aunt Lynne and friend

The Attitude of Gratitude

"Give thanks in all circumstances; for this is
the will of God in Christ Jesus for you."
1 Thessalonians 5:18 (ESV)

God bless you and your family on Thanksgiving. We remember those who are heavily burdened and yet joyful. As we partake of the Thanksgiving blessings, remember to pray for one another.

I am learning something surprising about gratitude, the steady drive of every part of life. The attitude of gratitude affects not only us and others, but it determines how life will work. Circumstances do not drive us; gratitude does, particularly thankfulness for Jesus.

Our Bible verse points out that we are to be thankful in difficult times. This is God's will for us in Jesus Christ. This verse does not demand perfect behavior. Instead, Jesus is an inviting Savior, not a ruthless and demanding dictator. He loves you and is with you every step of the way. This is the heart of intimacy, hand-in-hand together.

Challenge: Thank Jesus for something you have never thanked Him for. Again, ask God to bless those around you and to give you special healing, love and joy. Remember that we are serving Jesus Himself. Putting on Christ means that Christians are to be people of prayer, giving thanks. Only with prayer are relationships possible and harmonious.

Prayer: We come to You as family, to walk hand-in-hand with You as our head, "Our Father." I now know You love me, and I am filled with joy!

Love always,
Grandma, Aunt Lynne and friend

Stay Focused

"Your Word is a lamp unto my feet and a light unto my path."
Psalm 119:105 (KJV2000)

C *ome and I will show my path before you. My way shall become your way, the way that leads to life eternal. Do not lean on others but lean on Me, and I will give you strength and wisdom.*

I see all you want to accomplish, but you need to settle down and focus on Me. Only I can help direct your path step by step.

These steps are numbered, and day by day will I go before you. It can be so easy to become weary when your sights are way ahead. Take time to seek my presence and be filled with My Holy Spirit.

Challenge: Gradually your weariness will be exchanged with strength, and God's way will be made straight. Focus on the now — this is all we can do.

Prayer: I come, Lord, to be exonerated from all fear and let Your Son shine on my path.

Love always,
Grandma, Aunt Lynne and friend

Idolatry

"Where your treasure is, there your heart will be also."
Matthew 6:21 (NIV)

Jesus spoke these words to remind us that what we value, think about and work toward is what we love.

Idolatry is taking an incomplete joy of this world and building your entire life on it, essentially treasuring anything above Christ.

I've recently been asking the question, Do I have idols in my life? Things I would be lost without? I found these four questions to be a good test:

1) How important is _____ to me?
2) How often do I think about _____?
3) What do I get from _____?
4) How would I respond if _____ was taken away?

Nothing should be more significant to fill these blanks than my relationship with Jesus. If something does take precedence, then there's a strong chance I have an idol in my life.

An idol is often a good thing that becomes a *god* thing, then becomes a bad thing. And I think you will find they are more prevalent than we'd like to believe.

The most important thing to know is that an idol can't be removed; it can only be replaced.

Challenge: There's no use fighting to reduce idolatry in your life. The only true, lasting cure is replacing it with something even more desirable — something worth treasuring even more than image, money, success and reputation.

Prayer: Dear Lord, I pray You would truly be dear to my heart and be Lord of my life. I wage war against the little gods I've been going to for satisfaction. Help me to replace them with an all-consuming love for You. In Jesus' name, amen.

Love always,
Grandma, Aunt Lynne and friend

Depend on God

"For when I am weak, then I am strong."
2 Corinthians 12:10 (NIV)

M inistry is the core of the Christian life. We think we have to be strong, powerful, competent and smart.

Many think they have to reach a high level in terms of under-standing human behavior, but few are willing to lay down their own lives for others and make their own weakness a source of creativity for ministry.

Challenge: Ask yourself, am I willing to step out of the box and use my gifts and talents, without fear, to make myself available to others?

Prayer: Help me draw closer to Christ and the Holy Spirit as my source of strength, because serving others is where I want to direct my life. My question is, God, do You have a special area for me to serve in? For where You lead me, I will follow.

Love always,
Grandma, Aunt Lynne and friend

Life's Purpose

"Be still, and know that I am God."
Psalm 46:10 (ESV)

Going to the Lord is an on-going process. This life-long process of going to the Lord for direction and answers can affect the rest of your life.

Decisions concerning your friends, social circles, schools, dating, abstinence, your future mate, career and passions all require seeking, searching and praying.

We have to be careful not to run in circles like a monkey chasing his tail.

Many of my critical decisions were made between ages fourteen and twenty-five. I was first in my family to become a Christian and a college graduate, to marry a Christian and eventually dedicate our children to the Lord. I was then able to use my talents of music, art and writing to serve the Lord.

Challenge: May God be very close as you seek His will for your life. I pray God's Word becomes like a hand guide and direction map as you move forward with your life.

Prayer: I come to be anointed by You, Father, to serve and be led where I am to go now.

Love always,
Grandma, Aunt Lynne and friend

Habits

"Show me your ways, Lord, teach me your paths.
Guide me in your truth and teach me."
Psalm 25:4-5 (NIV)

The Bible instructs us to build healthy habits. Actions repeated without thinking will soon become natural to us. We must continually ask the Lord to show us the right path.

For instance, try putting your shirt on the arm opposite to what you would normally do. Not easy! Persist for twenty-one days, and you will have developed a new habit.

Challenge: Take a few focused minutes of silence with God. If done faithfully, it will set the stage for a more meaningful life. Or read one proverb on the corresponding day of the month. Billy Graham did this for many years, and a great habit was formed.

Prayer: I trust You, God, and will follow You. Help me form good habits and break bad habits.

Love always,
Grandma, Aunt Lynne and friend

We Are Chosen and Called His Friends

"You did not choose me, but I chose you and appointed you so that you
might go and bear fruit—fruit that will last—and so that whatever
you ask in my name the Father will give you."
John 15:16 (NIV)

*D*o *you take delight in Me, My child? For I am calling to you in
the night when all is still and you can hear My voice.*

*My coming to you will be soon, so faint not. Not only will I fill you
with light and glory, but My words will come to your heart speaking
very clearly what My purposes are for your life. Words of anointing
and words of direction.*

*So wait and see that I am good because you are precious to Me. I
have had plans for you since before you were in your mother's womb.*

Sometimes God's plans can affect thousands of generations. My
family is attesting to this promise.

Challenge: "Know therefore that the Lord your God is God; he is the
faithful God, keeping his covenant of love to a thousand generations
of those who love him and keep his commandments" (Deuteronomy
7:9, NIV).

Prayer: May Your words give me direction. I am open and now
come to You.

Love always,
Grandma, Aunt Lynne and friend

Life Can Be a Maze

"So whether you eat or drink or whatever you do, do it all for the
glory of God."
1 Corinthians 10:31 (NIV)

S ometimes God still is like a maze with only one way out and a
lot of dead ends. The most important issues for God are moral
purity, fidelity, compassion, joy, our witness, faithfulness, hospitality,
love, worship, forgiveness and faith. These are His concerns.

We should spend more time on all God has planned for us. Are
your motives, ethical decisions and choices right as you pursue life?

I think God is more concerned with our character, with *who we
are,* than whether we are a doctor or a lawyer.

Challenge: Be a servant and *walk humbly with God* (Micah 6:8,
paraphrased).

Prayer: "The Lord is my shepherd; I lack nothing. He makes me lie
down in green pastures, he leads me beside quiet waters, he refreshes
my soul. He guides me along the right paths for his name's sake"
(Psalm 23:1-3, NIV).

Love always,
Grandma, Aunt Lynne and friend

Perfect Peace

"You will keep in perfect peace all who trust in you,
all whose thoughts are fixed on you!"
Isaiah 26:3 (NLT)

I have a great desire to help you as you grow in Christ, and as I write I will wait until He gives me His words and ideas.

We can know perfect peace when we fix our thoughts on God even in turmoil. As we focus our minds on God and His Word, we become calm and stable. Supported by God's unchanging love and might, we are not downtrodden or surrounded by chaos.

Philippians 4:7 (NLT) says, if you do as He has commanded, "you will experience God's peace", which is far more wonderful than the human mind can comprehend. His peace will guard your heart and mind as you live in Christ Jesus.

Challenge: Let's turn our worries into prayers.

Prayer: God, help me to worry less. May I stop and pray. I have drawn the line in the sand, and I come to be surrounded by Your everlasting, loving arms. I long for you as in a thirsty land.

Love always,
Grandma, Aunt Lynne and friend

Remain in Him

"If you remain in me and my words remain in you,
ask whatever you wish and it will be given you."
John 15:7 (NIV)

*R*emain. Jesus chose this term to express the type of relationship He wants us to have with Him. *Remain* in His love. If we do that, He will remain in us, and our lives will be fruitful. Jesus wants us to know His Word, allowing it to funnel into our lives so it becomes our guide, a source of renewal and knowledge. *Remain in God*, and we will know we are in Him.

Challenge: Spend time with Him, get to know Him, be honest with Him and confess your sins. Do His will, and you will see answers to your prayers. Yes, do pray for yourself also.

Prayer: Help me, Lord, to hang on and thirst after righteousness. Let me *remain* in Your Word, seek Your guidance and know who I am in You. Speak to my heart, and I will follow.

Love always,
Grandma, Aunt Lynne and friend

You Are Not Alone

"For this command is a lamp, this teaching is a light, and correction
and instruction are the way to life."
Proverbs 6:23 (NIV)

No matter how hopeless life seems, God is there to help you take the next step. Now believe it, and the power of God will flood your heart and mind.

You see, God is real, and His presence is there for the asking. You may feel alone and that no one understands, but Jesus always does.

Challenge: Maybe life has not turned out the way you planned, but that's okay. God can free you to be the person He ordained you to be. Trust in His ways.

Prayer: I come now, God, to be filled with Your Holy Spirit and Your everlasting love. I believe—yes, I believe.

Love always,
Grandma, Aunt Lynne and friend

He Is My Rock

"He alone is my rock and my salvation,
my fortress where I will never be shaken."
Psalm 62:2 (NLT)

God, I am between a rock and a hard place! I have spent half the night trying to sleep, finish a paper and am agonizing over an injured knee. In other words, I am stuck!

In her blog article *9 Ways to Let Go of Stuck Thoughts*, Therese Borchard says, "Stuck thoughts [and behavior are like] the brick walls that form a prison around one's mind. The harder you try to get rid of them, the more powerful they become." [9]

Challenge: What do we do with these thoughts? Let's look at God's point of view and come to Him:

1) These thoughts will pass and are not permanent.
2) Focus on Jesus. Have that conversation you have been putting off and do it now.
3) Visualize walking with Christ and then get on your knees with your concerns and heart and pray.

Prayer: I come to You, O Lord, knowing I am in Your presence and heart. Again come into my heart and cleanse my thoughts and unrighteousness. Again I thank You.

Love always,
Grandma, Aunt Lynne and friend

Scoop! Life Is Not Always an Emergency

"When you pass through the waters, I will be with you; and when you pass through the rivers, they will not sweep over you. When you walk through the fire, you will not be burned; the flames will not set you ablaze."
Isaiah 43:2 (NIV)

S coop! The story of the year 2014! Snow, snow, snow!

What do we do when real hazardous conditions happen in our lives?

1) Stop, and *be still, and know that He is God* (Psalm 46:10, ESV, paraphrased).

2) Find a comfortable position and relax. Breathe in God and exhale confusion!

3) Ask for God's wisdom for He will give it abundantly.

4) Proceed knowing God is with you!

I wrote this just before I went into the hospital emergency room when a mid-winter storm was treacherous and no cars were on the road. Somewhat fearful, God blessed me with unknown friends who prayed numerous times with expectant healing hearts and hands. The staff, my family and, yes, the snow plows guaranteed my healing process.

Challenge: Let God touch you during storms of life and life-threatening conditions. Then you will find healing and restoration.

Prayer: Take us out of the storms of life, encourage us and help us move forward to Your light and strength.

Love always,
Grandma, Aunt Lynne and friend

You Have a Destiny, a Purpose

[Inspired by T. D. Jakes's *Instinct*] [10]
"I am the Way, the Truth, and the Life: No man cometh
unto the Father, but by me."
John 14:6 (KJV)

Now is the time to align your inner instincts, wisdom and action to who you really are. Acknowledge God's inner DNA to guide you toward what you are meant to do. This urgent message whispering within you can be called *drive*.

Many of you are in college or the work force or engaged in life's study to research what lies within. . .it never stops.

I'd like to share an example from my life. Besides being a wife and mother of four children, I was a Christian musician in many different avenues and had taught choir and sang solos for numerous years. Later in life I lost my voice unexpectedly, but that was okay because God opened up the fields of painting and writing. Great-grandmother Josepha P. Granger, at ninety years old, asked the same question. *What is my purpose? God, what is Your will for my life?* So you are not alone.

Challenge: Combine your unique gift with God, and the puzzle will begin to unfold. This is the life we are called to live. Allow excitement to fill you because you alone have a vision, a purpose and a gift you can bring to the world.

Prayer: God, if I fail in a particular area, help me and don't let depression sneak in the back door. Continue teaching me that researching what is inside me can be more fulfilling than any accomplishment. You have made me uniquely, so help me believe it!

Love always,
Grandma, Aunt Lynne and friend

Original painting by Lynne Granger

Instinctive Decision

[Inspired by T. D. Jakes's *Instinct*]
"Those who love their life in this world will lose it. Those who care
nothing for their life in this world will keep it for eternity."
John 12:25 (NLT)

We have a compass within us that guides us from where we are to where we are going. As T. D. Jakes teaches in his book *Instinct*, a wellspring of wisdom within not only helps you survive but can also help you thrive. [11]

Prayer and Challenge: Help me to find the quiet within me so I can listen and feel that which You have called me to be. God, speak to my heart. I need You, God, to help me sort out what You have called me to be. Release the roadblocks that keep me from You. Lead me to the place deep within me, my core, that place You have ordained. I want to sup with You, and sit with You, God. I know our instincts bear the imprint from the divine. I come from the road less traveled from the darkness to the light.

Love always,
Grandma, Aunt Lynne and friend

What You Focus on Will Dominate You

"Fix your thoughts on what is true, and honorable,
and right, and pure, and lovely, and admirable. Think about things
that are excellent and worthy of praise."
Philippians 4:8 (NLT)

Are you excited and walking in the manifestations of His grace? Focus and give attention to His promises. It's not what people say, but what Jesus has already done. Do not focus on problems today; do not make a list in your head. Instead, focus on truth and all He has done for you: I am delivered, healed, joyful, loved and forgiven.

Consider that whatever you focus on will dominate you. Meditate daily on the Lord because the world is competing for your attention. Yes, this is a struggle; like war, we need the armor of God!

Challenge: Focus on God's truth and not on that of the world. Remember His promises, presence and grace. Attend to God's Word. Hear it, think it and live it obediently, in Christ's power.

Prayer: God, help me remember Your promises and seek Your presence and grace.

Love always,
Grandma, Aunt Lynne and friend

Encouragement

"You will arise and have compassion on Zion, for it is time to show favor to her; the appointed time has come."
Psalm 102:13 (NIV)

D ear loved ones, I write this letter to encourage you and let you know that God loves you and is with you throughout these days before the Christmas season.

You are special, you are terrific, you are wonderful, I am proud of you, and God has His hand on you. This is the first day of the rest of your life. Maybe hard times have held you down for a while, but look up and become the person God has created you to be!

Obstacles will make you come out strong, more determined, and with greater faith than you have ever had before. God is not limited by our disbelief. What is your fear? The economy, your education and exams, your health, disappointments, friends, your future spouse or family?

Psalm 102:13 says there is a set time for favor (NIV). God has a set time for increase and favor. These are seasons when God will open supernatural increase and blessings. Supernatural doors will open, and you will accomplish things you never thought possible, in seasons you thought would never happen! Remember a seed planted in the spring will not produce a harvest until the end of the summer, another season.

Jesus said the *Spirit of the Lord is upon me to help the poor, to comfort the hurting, and to declare the year of God's favor* (Isaiah 61:1-2, ESV, paraphrased). You see, we are serving a supernatural God. Deep down something says, *yes, this is for me! God is a God of abundance, and this is for me.*

Challenge: "May the God of hope fill you with all joy and peace in believing through the experience of your faith that you may abound and be overflowing with hope" (Romans 15:13, ESV).

Prayer: May I be a shining light during this season of hope and joy. I will not be down-spirited but lifted up so others can see Your face.

Love always,
Grandma, Aunt Lynne and friend

My Prayer IV

"For God will break the chains that bind His people."
Isaiah 9:4 (TLB)

You are real, God. I know it. I can see it on the faces of my loved ones and those who surround me. Come and lift me out of my dirty clay; break the chains that bind me and please make me whole. I have come to be free of this heaviness and loneliness. I long for Your truth, the truth of the healer, Jesus! Set me free and make me the kind of person You want me to be! I long for You as if in a dry and thirsty land. Fill my cup, Lord; fill it up and make me whole!

This is a message of hope that God would shine His light on everyone living in the shadow of death. He is both *Wonderful Counselor* and *Mighty God*. This message was fulfilled in Christ and His establishment of His eternal kingdom. He came to deliver all people from slavery and sin.

Love always,
Grandma, Aunt Lynne and friend

God's Plans Are Greater

"We can make our own plans, but the Lord gives the right answer. . .we
can make our own plans, but the Lord determines our steps."
Proverbs 16:1, 9 (NLT)

Is school or life hard? Did you take a test, fail it and have a panic attack? This happened to me during finals, and I ended up crying my eyes out. This experience not only changed the direction but the course of my life. I did not drop my music major but instead resolved to dedicate my field to Christ and to working on Christian music.

God used what I had (and not what I did not have), multiplied my gift and used it for His glory.

Challenge: Let God use who you are. Give Him what He has given you so you can produce good fruit. Something hard can be turned into joy. Open your mind.

Prayer: I love You, God, with an everlasting love, and I put my hand in Yours.

Love always,
Grandma, Aunt Lynne and friend

Rest in Me

"Have mercy on me, Lord; heal me, for I have sinned against you."
Psalm 41:4 (NIV)

*N*ow *follow me as I have called you from the dark to rise up and greet the morn. You are My child, and I love you with a love so deep and wide. A love so encompassing that only those who hear My voice will stop and listen.*

Even when life seems hard, I am here to serve you and to encompass you with my everlasting loving arms. Again, be still and know that I am yours. A God that not only tends to His sheep but tends to His sons and daughters.

Challenge: Believe when God says, *I will freely give you peace. A peace that abides, all the peace that only the Holy Spirit can give.*

Prayer: Lord, help me rest in You and quiet my breathing. Come—I beckon you.

Love always,
Grandma, Aunt Lynne and friend

The Joy of the Lord Is Your Strength

"Don't be dejected and sad. The joy of the Lord is your strength."
Nehemiah 8:10 (NLT)

My child, fear not, for the pain will dispatch, and the glory of the morn will encompass you. You are My child, and I will love you to the end of the ages. I will draw all men unto Me for they shall be filled with light. Many will know Me because you have come.

You seem weary; but I will fill you with My presence, and you will be filled with the joy of the Lord. His joy is your strength.

Pass on what has been given you and walk together down the road God has set before you. You are My child so walk also with Me. Be glad and rejoice always.

Challenge: God loves you, so pass it on.

Prayer: Again I lift myself to You, O Christ.

Love always,
Grandma, Aunt Lynne and friend

Choose Me

[Inspired by T. D. Jakes's *Instinct*]
"Create in me a pure heart, O God, and renew a steadfast spirit
within me."
Psalm 51:10 (NIV)

I n reading T. D. Jakes's book *Instinct*, pages 24-27, I have found that we should follow our instincts. This will drive you beyond what you would expect in your life. [12]

We all have access to the same information and opportunities, but some of us never go beyond what is required.

Let's combine instincts with intellect to discover a new way of seeing what's missing in plain sight. Don't push, go to a certain point and stop.

We are talking about creativity. Don't limit yourself, but push on into new waters of the divine. God made us to reflect His purpose and fulfillment. He wants us to see beyond the literal, above the bottom line and beneath the surface of appearances.

Challenge: Become what you are meant to be. Resonate the challenge before you, where creativity resonates with the horizon of possibility.

Prayer: God, unlock the door to the larger life—works and cravings of the inner soul. Help me to keep going and not stop. Amen!

Love always,
Grandma, Aunt Lynne and friend

Christmas Love

"He anointed us, set his seal of ownership on us, and put his Spirit in our hearts as a deposit, guaranteeing what is to come."
2 Corinthians 1:21-22 (NIV)

I thought I would share some lines from some Christmas cards –

Celebrate the journey. "Thanks be to God for His indescribable gift!" (2 Corinthians 9:15, NIV)

Jesus the faithful one
The confidence we have…
The trust we hold…
The hope we carry
Rest in His faithfulness
Every promise He has made
His purpose to fulfill
He has the authority to accomplish all He has spoken
His power is limitless
His character is changeless
His love is endless

As He gave His life for us, may we live each day out of love for Him. I hope your Christmas is blessed with the joy of knowing how very precious you are to Jesus.

Challenge: Share the love of Christ with someone else today as you meditate on Christ's love for you.

Prayer: Thank You, God, that we can celebrate the greatest gift, the birth of Jesus Christ.

Love always,
Grandma, Aunt Lynne and friend

Be Calm Within

"The Spirit gives life."
John 6:63 (NIV)

B e calm even though the treacherous storm rages around you. Be still and seek His presence deep within. Wait, allow the love and Spirit to rise up within you, and you will be blessed.

Does the "beat" within you pound and pound? You were made for His glory, so slow down and be in sync with that which you were made to be.

Yes, you are very special, and God will march along right beside you. Yes, you are meant for His glory. So again I say, what is this literal beat? Nearness to God.

Brother Lawrence said to practice the presence of God. [13] As a monk, he practiced this presence silently while peeling potatoes all day long. God will not fail you. Listen to His voice and draw deep within you. Only then will you find your true self.

Challenge: God says, "I have come that you might have life and have it more abundantly" (John 10:10, KJV). Will you trust Him? Can you find time to practice the presence of God?

Prayer: I love You, Lord. In the stillness and quietness shall I know You, the loving God.

Love always,
Grandma, Aunt Lynne and friend

The Golden Rule

"So in everything do to others what you would have them do to you, for this sums up the Law and the Prophets."
Matthew 7:12 (NIV)

Many of us learned to recite the Golden Rule as a child. Treat others as you would want to be treated. If you want respect, treat others with respect.

The Golden Rule as Jesus formulated it is the foundation of active goodness and mercy—the kind of love He shows us every day. By stating it positively, Jesus made the initiative and does something good for others because this is a healthy decision. Are you following this rule as an adult? As a Spirit-filled believer, you must take the initiative to treat people the way you would like to be treated, not the way they treat you.

This Golden Rule is the foundation of our family business. It has been like a ripple in a pond that gets wider and wider.

Challenge: The Golden Rule is not a manipulative action, but a heartfelt decision to live. It has a rhythm of its own as your heart has the beat of your life. Choose to live by this rhythm today.

Prayer: God, help me follow You, and please direct my life!

Love always,
Grandma, Aunt Lynne and friend

Keep on Your Toes

"Keep company with me and you'll learn to live freely and lightly."
Matthew 11:29-30 (MSG)

Do you find it hard to say, "I don't know"? I was raised to believe that one person always had to be right. My husband cut me short when I couldn't say, "I don't know!"

I then began to enjoy the freedom to say, "I don't know," and became free from worry, burdens and overload. It was refreshing when I realized I didn't have to know everything about everything.

Turn to God for the heavy stuff because He is all-knowing and in control. Still confused? Seek a counselor, a professor, a friend or parent. That's what they are there for.

Challenge: Keep company with God, trust Him and keep on your toes so you learn to live freely.

Prayer: Help me realize, God, that I don't need to know everything about everything.

Love always,
Grandma, Aunt Lynne and friend

Wait on the Lord

"But those who hope in the Lord will renew their strength. They will soar
on wings like eagles; they will run and not grow weary;
they will walk and not be faint."
Isaiah 40:31 (NIV)

This waiting business is like putting on a new self. It simply means:

Spending time with God

Being in His presence

Meditating on His Word

Worshipping Him

Keeping Him at the center of your life

When you wait on the Lord, you receive everything you need to live a victorious life. He is your source, so remember that nothing can separate you from the love of Jesus (Romans 8:38-39).

Challenge: Wait on the Lord each and every day and do whatever He asks you to do.

Prayer: God, this waiting business is tough, and I am not afraid of the work. Fill me with love, healing and peace.

Love always,
Grandma, Aunt Lynne and friend

My Heart Is Yours

"I rejoiced greatly in the Lord that at last you renewed your
concern for me."
Philippians 4:10 (NIV)

O n my fifty-second anniversary of marriage, I greet the morn
and my steps are marked before me. I am Yours, O God.
Please take away that which is earthly in me—my pain and distrac-
tions—and fill me with Your Holy Spirit and, yes, Your love.

I long for You as if in a dry land. Come and lift me up to a better
place, Your place, Your anointing.

I am so thirsty, and my lips are parched with longing. You alone
can satisfy my thirst. My longing is for You to take me from this
place and put Your everlasting arms around me. God, You alone
can make this earthly dwelling, my little corner, Your place too. My
heart is Yours, my life is Yours, and these college kids and grand-
kids are Yours.

Challenge: Seek hope, and you will find life.

Prayer: God, let these young people know that if some of this world
is upsetting this is only a part of the whole picture. May they not lose
hope. Hope is their girding and life-line.

Love always,
Grandma, Aunt Lynne and friend

The God Factor

"Lean on, trust in, and be confident in the Lord with all your heart and mind and do not rely on your own insight or understanding."
Proverbs 3:5 (AMP)

Are you a person who wants to be involved in everything? When we try to do everything, we don't do anything well. Quality is better than quantity. Don't neglect present duties by taking on new ones. Don't act emotionally without forethought.

Life would be so much better if we all took time to think about what we are about to do before we do it. Not everything that looks good *is good*, and a wise person will take time to examine things thoroughly. Don't settle for another thing, but choose the more excellent thing.

The God factor is knowing what God has called you to do and sticking with His call. This will save you from burn out, unnecessary activities and wasting resources. It will also give you confidence and allow you to focus on and organize the little and big things.

We all have different levels of energy, health and allotted time to manage. We want to do the very best in the things we accomplish, and that does not mean pulling an "all-nighter" or putting things off. I can't help but think of a turtle and its steady pace to reach its goal.

Knowing God has called you, you can trust God's hand will be on you and your decisions.

Challenge: Remember: when an appointment comes up carefully consider how it will affect your present duties before you commit.

Prayer: I give You my heart and mind. Help me lean on and trust in You.

Love always,
Grandma, Aunt Lynne and friend

Dread

"Don't put it off; do it now! Don't rest until you do."
Proverbs 6:4 (NLT)

Do you dread little things or major things more?

Like many of you, I have a lot to do, and it does not do any good to constantly dread the little things. It steals my joy, and I am not willing to live that way. The more you conquer the little things, the better prepared spiritually you become for the bigger things.

I made a decision I would do these things joyfully and exercise my self-control and faith muscles God has given me.

You can have that too by not allowing fear and dread to rule in your lives. Practice walking in faith, and each time will be easier and easier.

I spent a lot of my life in fear and worry because I did not know God. I did not trust God to come through for me. Things are different now seeing that I can look to God for help.

Challenge: Refuse to give up. Take hold of and practice walking in faith. The more you practice, the bigger your faith muscle becomes.

Prayer: I claim Proverbs 6:4, and I say it again, "Don't put it off; do it now! Don't rest until you do" (NLT).

Love always,
Grandma, Aunt Lynne and friend

Separation

"These things I have spoken to you, that my joy may be in you,
and that your joy may be full."
John 15:11 (ESV)

S eparation abounds—parent from child, friend from friend, and dreams from adult realities. But there is a separation committed Christians will never have to face—separation from Jesus' unfailing love.

I have endeavored to show the truth of God by studying more than three-dozen resources—the King James Bible, the New Application Bible, Stewardship Study Bible, the Grandmother's Bible, and many articles and online resources. We must all study to show ourselves approved. I hope my writing skills will continue to improve.

Challenge: Our Christian legacy can be worn and tattered, but we can choose to change and be responsible for our families, friends and the workplace. Jesus chose us, so let us choose God's love and kindness toward Him and our neighbors.

Prayer: Light up my path each step of the way, because I choose You, God, my King, my Redeemer, my Savior.

Love always,
Grandma, Aunt Lynne and friend

Christmas–Born Again

"The Word became flesh and made his dwelling among us."
John 1:14 (NIV)

Even before our birth God prepared a special place for Jesus to be "born again" in us—not physically, but in a spiritual sense. That's why we can celebrate both birthdays all year long: ours, and the one for our Savior. Christmas is more, so much more, than a holiday. And it's even more than the birthday of Jesus. The true spirit of Christmas begins the moment we invite Jesus into our hearts; it lasts more than one day or one season. The spirit keeps on going and going and going. The Word became flesh through Jesus and now *lives in us*. How exciting that now, after Jesus' birth, death and resurrection, Jesus continues the preparation God began.

Challenge: As you make your preparations for Christmas this year, remember to prepare your heart in grateful celebration for the One who wants to live in every person.

Prayer: I would like to celebrate my birthday today as a child of God.

Love always,
Grandma, Aunt Lynne and friend

Kindness

"But the fruit of the Spirit is love, joy, peace, forbearance, kindness, goodness, faithfulness, gentleness and self-control."
Galatians 5:22-23 (NIV)

There are different fruits of the Spirit, kindness being one of them. *My ways can be your ways, so be kind to one another so others will be drawn to Me.* This simple act will show love toward others, and your strength will enlarge.

When our sin nature dies, we are given new life in Jesus. We undergo radical changes, and pre-occupation with old interests clouds like vapor. Power, prestige, popularity and the desire to accumulate wealth fade, and suddenly we do not want the same things anymore. We now desire grace, His love and the manifestation of the Holy Spirit.

I have chosen kindness because my husband emulates it, as he is not only there for me, but our family and the Lord.

The Lord beckons us to seek the better things.

Challenge: Do you know there are many gifts? Some are for the asking, and some are not. Check out Galatians 5; Ephesians 4; 1 Corinthians 12, 13 and 14; and James 5.

Prayer: Help me to be patient and kind toward family, friends, those in authority, and the person on the street. Fill me with compassion, kindness and love.

Love always,
Grandma, Aunt Lynne and friend

Keep in Step

"Since we live by the Spirit, let us keep in step with the Spirit."
Galatians 5:25 (NIV)

God, my desire is to be who You have called me to be. Some things disturb me in this step-by-step journey like confusion, pain and endurance. Impulses.

Daily may I be transformed by the renewing and infilling of the Holy Spirit. Christ has crucified my sinful nature with its passions and desires.

An effective steward will above all do everything out of love — love for God, love for others, love for the church, love for creation.

You will exhibit the fruit of the Spirit more and more as you mature, showing love, joy, peace, patience, kindness, goodness, faithfulness, gentleness and self-control. Against such things there is no law.

Challenge: We shall no longer be slaves to our sinful nature and can be renewed so we can reap what we sow (Galatians 6:7, NIV).

Prayer: Lord, knowing what I am holding back, please help me to relinquish selfishness and turn it into kindness.

Love always,
Grandma, Aunt Lynne and friend

Off-Beat Day

"For God is not a God of confusion but of peace."
1 Corinthians 14:33 (ESV)

Yesterday was an off-beat day, and I couldn't make simple decisions. I became confused and disoriented; then I became physically ill and suddenly had to turn off and go to bed.

The next morning things became clearer, but I still had to make many decisions. This verse became my guideline, and confusion no longer became an option.

I gave my heart to God, and His understanding became my will. Now I am with anticipation and can rest in Him.

Challenge: Let go and let God.

Prayer: Father, help me lean on You and trust and acknowledge that You are in charge. I love You and will walk Your path step-by-step with You.

Love always,
Grandma, Aunt Lynne and friend

What Lasts

"The grass withers and the flowers fall, but the word of our God endures forever."
Isaiah 40:8 (NIV)

I remember being struck by Isaiah 40:8 when our son Todd gave me a plaque with this verse. This is a sobering perspective on priorities and what lasts forever.

Ask yourself, *Is faith really important in my life?*

It is easy to run after worldly things—a large house, the next big internship or promotion. Some strive to gain a large portfolio, while others look to having their names in lights. These earthly gains will not last. They will fade.

Challenge: Look deeply inside yourself and be still. You are on your way to knowing God's prize. It is by His wisdom, power, counsel and control that you can find His leading. While you are seeking, He says to you, "Do not fear." I myself "will uphold you with my righteous right hand" (Isaiah 41:10, NIV).

Prayer: Father, help me look within, so I may follow Your leading and not worldly passions.

Love always,
Grandma, Aunt Lynne and friend

What Is Ministry?

"Your labor prompted by love, and your endurance inspired by hope in
our Lord Jesus Christ. . .[because] He has chosen you."
1 Thessalonians 1:3-4 (NIV)

Ministry is being a blessing. It is serving and giving and not counting the cost. It's a spiritual act.

Ministry is a full-time, twenty-four-hour thing. This is why I can't wait to get up in the morning. I can't believe I have the privilege of doing this thing. It is an emptying and filling to overflowing. Yeah, Jesus!

Ministry is for all of us, whether we were raised in church or came to know Christ outside the church.

Challenge: Don't say you haven't any opportunities or training. Determine this week how you might give of yourself to someone who needs you.

Prayer: Jesus, please show me the many opportunities to serve that are right in front of me every day.

Love always,
Grandma, Aunt Lynne and friend

Thank You for This Day

"The Lord is my shepherd, I lack nothing. He makes me lie down in
green pastures,
he leads me beside quiet waters, he refreshes my soul."
Psalm 23:1-3 (NIV)

Dear heavenly Father, beside the still waters I come to be filled.
What a wonderful day You have provided. It is so good I have
chosen You to be with me every step of the way, knowing I only have
to ask and Your comforting still, small voice is always there.

I love You, God. Please teach me to be calm and let the tension
go, so I know the breeze I feel outside between classes is Your Holy
Spirit comforting me.

A hole in my heart needs to be filled. Teach me to stop now and
breathe in Your healing.

Challenge: God, help me to come to You, and may this act become
a habit all the days of my life.

Prayer: Thank You for that special person who led me to Your presence and still waters. You are important to me, and I trust what You
have said to me and future generations.

Love always,
Grandma, Aunt Lynne and friend

You Count

"Where you go I will go, and where you stay I will stay. Your people will
be my people and your God my God."
Ruth 1:16 (NIV)

Every one of us counts. Ruth, an outsider and immigrant, was a key player in God's story. Because of her obedience she became a great-grandmother of King David and an ancestor of Jesus.

God still has a plan even when life is hard. He can come in, break you, shake things up, introduce new options and then restore you. *Sadness can turn to joy* (Jeremiah 31:13, NIV, paraphrased).

Challenge: Be under God's protective wing and thank Him for picking you up and treating you kindly as His chosen people. Seek His face and receive His promise, Jesus Christ.

Prayer: Bless my family and friends as they seek and develop the talents You have given them. Help them, as well as myself, to be thankful and confident as we grow closer to You.

Love always,
Grandma, Aunt Lynne and friend

The Silent God

"My soul thirsts for God, for the living God. When can I go and meet
with God? My tears have been my food day and night."
Psalm 42:2-3 (NIV)

There may be times in life when, after thirsting for God, weeping
for His help and enduring ridicule, He still remains silent (Psalm
42:1-3, NIV).

Such times often lead to depression and discouragement, but
there is a remedy.

1) Remember God's blessings in your life.
2) Although God seems silent, He is there and will once again
   receive your praise.
3) Gaze again upon God's beautiful creation that proclaims His
   love (Psalm 42:6-8, NLT).
4) The psalmist felt blows of sorrow but realized he was never
   adrift from God's steadfast love (Psalm 42:7-8, NIV).
5) Faithfully expect God to act. Do this, and you will once again
   find reason to praise Him!

Take courage, my loved ones, and when you cannot seem to find
God, use this remedy and God will help you. This will give you hope.
Our lives depend on this. You will not rest until your relationship
with God has been restored.

This will help you to rely on God's ability rather than on your
own inability.

When you are down, take advantage of this psalm's anti-depressant.

Challenge: God will be your remedy and hope!

Prayer: I am discouraged and, yes, depressed. I find I need You, God,
so very, very much. And again I seek Your counsel.

Love always,
Grandma, Aunt Lynne and friend

Easter Morn

"Do not be afraid, for I know that you are looking for Jesus, who was crucified. He is not here; he has risen, just as he said."
Matthew 28:5-6 (NIV)

I come to greet you and share the love Christ has given to me and to all men. I have written this letter four times and decided I would write from the heart instead.

His biggest blessing is our sharing Christ and His resurrection. God is so good. If you are out of sorts, you must connect with God's greatest gift, His Son, who died on the cross for you and for me. This is the greatest gift of all! Just think—we can be free from the chains that bind us. Can you make this step and ask God to fill you full of His presence?

I know some of you are lonely and concerned about your future. *How can I make my resume look good?* God wants you to listen to your heart and be obedient. I never get tired of the verse "Be still, and know I am God" (Psalm 46:10, ESV). This was the first verse I ever memorized, and it still works for me! His presence is in those words.

"Come to Me, all who are weary and heavy-laden, and I will give you rest. Take My yoke upon you and learn from me. . .For My yoke is easy, and My burden is light" (Matthew 11:28-30, NASB).

He is here now! Believe! But you have to take the first step. "This is the day that the Lord has made; let us rejoice and be glad in it" (Psalm 118:24, ESV).

You are not alone.

To Him be the power, glory and honor forever!

Challenge: Trust in Him always. Do not be full of fear, cynicism, mocking and jeering. Be faithful; be faithful to the end. Remember that what you say is what you are. Be reciprocators of "I am" because He is.

Prayer: God, I come to praise You, as You are the one true God. And I come to praise You for Your Son, Jesus, who died on the cross, and His resurrection is our life.

Love always,
Grandma, Aunt Lynne and friend

Not Just Surviving

[Inspired by T. D. Jakes's *Instinct*] [14]
"That person is like a tree planted by streams of water, which yields its
fruit in season and whose leaf does not wither—
whatever they do prospers."
Psalm 1:3 (NIV)

Y ou cannot keep a good person down. When you honor God with
your life, when you are a person of integrity and excellence,
you have the blessing of God. Just like cream, you will rise to the
top. Hold your head up high, not in arrogance, but in confidence. No
matter whether you are at school, home, in the cafeteria, at the store,
or in your room, you can be a blessing.

God wants you to be so blessed that when other people see you
they will want what you have. You may not be in the perfect place
now, but remind yourself, *I am blessed. Goodness and mercy are
following me right now. God is supporting me with His love and
everlasting arms.* Your days of surviving are over, and your days of
thriving have just begun!

Psalm 1:2-3 says *if we keep God first, we will be like a tree
planted by the waters. Our leaves will not wither. This is like an
oasis where you will bear much fruit* (NIV). The fruit of the Spirit is
"love, joy, peace, patience, kindness, goodness, faithfulness, gentleness, and self-control" (Galatians 5:22-23, NLT).

Challenge: Deep down you can know you're blessed by God. Make
this decision with me and say, *I am not just surviving, because this
is my year to thrive!* Let go of the past and let God lead. His way is
a lot easier and full of light. My mistakes are there to help me move
on and ahead.

Prayer: Bless me, Lord, with goodness and mercy, and thank You
for Your favor.

Love always,
Grandma, Aunt Lynne and friend

Wisdom

"Get wisdom, get understanding; do not forget my words
or turn away from them."
Proverbs 4:5 (NIV)

At times we feel cut off from God. We feel lonely, needing more of His power, presence and companionship. Or could it be we do not know what we want?

This year we are concentrating on "I choose." This is another opportunity to draw nigh unto Him. We can read and memorize the Scriptures. For example, "Be still, and know that I am God" (Psalm 46:10, ESV). This verse is my very favorite. I try to do what it says—and soon I am in His presence and no longer alone!

Are you concerned about your future and the direction of your life? Turn to Proverbs 4, and God will speak to you of His wisdom. I will take a scripture like this and put it in my own words: Get wisdom, and you will get supreme understanding. Wisdom will protect you, watch over you and give you life, safety and honor. We who seek godly wisdom over earthly knowledge and ego-fame experience a river flowing out of us like water from a cup.

"When you walk, your steps will not be hampered; when you run, you will not stumble" (Proverbs 4:12, NIV). "Above all else, guard your heart" against evil (Proverbs 4:23, NIV). "But the path of the righteous is like the light of dawn, which shines brighter and brighter" (Proverbs 4:18, ESV).

My sons and daughters, pay attention and listen closely to my words. *Continue to guard them in your heart for they are life to those who find them and health to the whole body* (Proverbs 4:20-22, NLT, paraphrased). *Always keep corrupt and perverse talk from your lips. Look straight ahead and make level paths for your feet* (Proverbs 4:24-25, NTL, paraphrased).

He is God, so do not faint. Sleep well, and tomorrow will be a new day. You will find you are not alone. It is well, it is well with my soul!

Challenge: I encourage you to bathe yourself with the promises and warnings of Proverbs 4, for it is a roadmap of good advice. Seek His truth and live. So memorize and study. *I choose wisdom.*

Prayer: God, You say if we seek wisdom, You will give it generously without rebuke (James 1:5, ISV).

Love always,
Grandma, Aunt Lynne and friend

How Good God Is

"Here I am, I have come. . .I desire to do your will, my God;
your law is within my heart."
Psalm 40:7-8 (NIV)

To you all I give thanks, for God is molding you, and you can be lifted up if you just call upon His name.

As I read the psalms (Psalm 40 in particular, which I read before some of you were born), I find that devotion to God is life's calling—our choicest accomplishment. This takes devotion without selfishness. Remember that obedience is better than sacrifice (1 Samuel 15:22, NIV). Samuel asked three times, "Here I am. Did you call me?" (1 Samuel 3:4, NLT). Make sure you give God the obedience and lifelong service He desires from you. Needless to say, Samuel followed after the Lord and is remembered by all to this day!

Remember that all you have to do is say, *Yes, Lord! Do not delay; come quickly; save me.* He is our Savior.

You all are of my heart, and I love you. You need not fear for the morrow.

Prayer: Thank You for forgiving my sins, and may I tell others the good news. May I not hide this in my heart, but may I tell my friends. Fill me with the Holy Spirit to be bold, but with a gentle spirit. Help me pray for others when they are sick and on their bed with physical and emotional pain and also those who need help. Thank You for trying to bring me close to You into Your presence, thoughts, love and faithfulness.

Challenge: If God always has us in His thoughts, perhaps we could do more for Him. How good God is. As He has blessed us let us bless others. One or two good friends are worth more than one hundred friends not of the Lord.

Love always,
Grandma, Aunt Lynne and friend

My Prayer V

"Why am I discouraged? Why so sad? I will put my hope in God!
I will praise Him again—my Savior and my God!"
Psalm 42:11 (NLT)

Dear Lord, do not pass me by when I cry unto You. Even though I have not called You recently, I call You from the depths of my core because I really, really love You. I choose You above all else because You are real. With my heart I come again to be filled full of Your love, compassion and healing power.

Now I rise up to greet the morning because I have reason to have joy, and that is because You are with me. Blessed am I because Your strength fills me and I am made whole. I say thank You because You are filling me with Your strength and healing power, knowing I am free to be Yours.

Love always,
Grandma, Aunt Lynne and friend

Original painting by Lynne Granger

And It Was Good

"For you created my inmost being; you knit me together in my
mother's womb.
I praise you because I am fearfully and wonderfully made"
Psalm 139:13-14 (NIV)

I come to you with love of a bountiful heart. The Lord has given me
the ministry *College Kids,* which is now bearing fruit as *Living
Waters Prayer Letters* to all who read them. I have many thanksgivings and insights for giving Him glory and honor.

Last year it was a real struggle to write, but this year (my sixth year
of writing) He has given me so many resources: the Bible, books,
sermons, prayers and leadings from the Holy Spirit. I pray this will
help you grow spiritually, help us grow close into the family of God
and help you reach out with the fruit of the Spirit.

"You have searched me, Lord, and you know me. . . . You are
familiar with all my ways (Psalm 139:1, 3, NIV). His love for you is
without bounds. His provision for purpose for you is without measure. He chose and created you with purpose and ability! Do not
worry for the morrow.

For you created me in my mother's womb. . .you knitted me
(Psalm 139:13, NIV, paraphrased)—and it was good! "I praise you
because I am fearfully and wonderfully made" (Psalm 139:14, NIV).
It was good He chose your mother's womb. I had never thought of
that before. It makes my mom special. Think about that. He loves
you in all ways.

Challenge: Help me to sacrifice as my mother did for me, and help
me to be mindful of those times.

Prayer: God, thank You for choosing me even before I was born.

Love always,
Grandma, Aunt Lynne and friend

Murphy's Law vs. God's Law

"I delight in your law."
Psalm 119:70 (NIV)

H ave you ever made a mountain out of a molehill? Is there something in your life that you are blowing way out of proportion?

I would like to introduce you to the difference between Murphy's
law and God's law. Also the concept: *What you think is who you are.*

Murphy's law: If anything can go wrong, it will. How negative!
Who would want to live that way? Me! I grew up in an extremely
pessimistic home, and this law was the norm. All I heard was, *You
can't do this*, or *you are incapable of following your dreams*. I also
heard I could not date Jerry or go to college.

I did! This changed when I found Christ and discovered God's
law, which proclaimed: If anything can go right, it will! Nothing is
as difficult as it seems. If anything goes right, it will, and if anything
can happen to anybody, it can happen to you. God has a great plan
for you. So let your thinking and lifestyle connect to God, who is the
source and anchor for your life right now. Jesus wants you to enjoy
life to the fullest. Remember: What you think is who you are, and if
anything can go right or good, it will. God's law is forever.

Challenge: I challenge you to enjoy each and every day. Take three
areas of your life and look at it from God's law and perspective. Keep
a small journal or diary for the rest of the semester, and you will see
improvement.

Prayer: God, I accept this challenge, so I will get started by finding a
journal today! Three areas of my life are _____ , _____ , _____

Love always,
Grandma, Aunt Lynne and friend

Feed Your Faith with God's Word, So Life Tastes Good

"Man shall not live on bread alone, but on every word
that comes from the mouth of God."
Matthew 4:4 (NIV)

D o you ever try something, and then it blows up in your face? This happens to me often enough so that I have to center myself once again in God.

I can quiet myself by saying, "Be still, and know that I am God" (Psalm 46:10, ESV). I keep coming back to this verse because it is so powerful. I stop what I am doing, take a slow deep breath and repeat the verse. I center myself with calm and His power, and, yes, I am better!

I have problems with guilt. This can develop into nervousness and confusion to the place where I am almost numb. I had to ask God to come into my life and by His power free me from Satan's hold. We have to free ourselves from these moments by quoting Scripture.

Look in your concordance for verses reflecting your need; then write out the Scripture verse and commit it to memory. It is powerful, and there comes a moment when we are free of guilt and shame. Breathe slowly in class, at night, and your worry will be replaced by His presence.

Declare that *by His stripes you are healed!* (Isaiah 53:5, KJV, paraphrased). Declare that "perfect love casts out [all] fear!" (1 John 4:18, ESV). Declare that "God. . .will supply all your needs" (Philippians 4:19, NLT). Declare that *because you are born of God, you have faith to overcome the world!* (1 John 5:4, ESV, paraphrased).

Challenge: Store words of God in your heart and mind today so you can declare them in times of need or praise. Remember to feed your faith with God's words so life tastes good.

Prayer: I come to be bathed in Your Word so it can be life to my body and food for my soul.

Love always,
Grandma, Aunt Lynne and friend

He Has a Good Plan for Your Life

"'For I know the plans I have for you,' declares the Lord, 'plans to prosper you and not to harm you, plans to give you hope and a future.'"
Jeremiah 29:11 (NIV)

N ow you are home, along with green trees, mosquitoes and storms. Storms take many forms: sprinkles, tumultuous storms and sunny storms. If you are like me, storms are good and exciting, but some are not so good yet seem ever-present.

I have been clinging to Jeremiah 29:11 because sometimes life's purposes can be on the back burner. Great-Grandmother told me about her search for purpose in February 1999, when she was in her nineties. She said, "In my spiritual life, please, God, give me a clear vision far into the future, and for today, of what I am to do. Abraham trusted God to lead him. . .me too, God, and thanks! The Lord will give me strength to keep me going, and that is all you can do." — Josephina H. Granger

I have drawn a picture around her quote with a photo of three generations. If a grandchild or anyone else is ever troubled with this age-long question, I show them this simple picture.

Challenge: Please memorize Jeremiah 29:11 along with me.

Prayer: God, I seek Your will for my life.

Love always,
Grandma, Aunt Lynne and friend

Ask for Boldness to Share Your Faith

"I pray that you may be active in sharing your faith."
Philemon 6 (NIV)

The moment we meet Jesus for the first time, our lives are changed forever. It is a moment we never forget. Why, then, is it so hard to introduce Him to friends and family? After all, this will change their lives forever. Jesus saves us, transforms our lives and gives us the privilege of being a part of someone else's salvation. We fear we might be nervous and pressured or that we will say something wrong and turn someone off entirely.

Sharing our faith is a divine calling and furthers the work of God, but we cannot do it without God's power. We need to ask God for opportunities to talk about Jesus and communicate His love in such a way that people will understand His salvation and be attracted to His love.

Challenge: Pray often that you will be able to share your faith whenever the opportunity presents itself and that God will give you the perfect words to say. Pray for God to soften the hearts of those you speak to so they can receive the truth.

Prayer: God, help me to get over any inhibitions I have about sharing my faith with unbelievers. Help me to have a perfect sense of timing, the right words to say and, most of all, the infilling of the Holy Spirit. I love You!

Love always,
Grandma, Aunt Lynne and friend

Fear Not

"Fear not, for I am with you; be not dismayed, for I am your God; I will
strengthen you, I will help you, I will uphold you with my righteous
right hand."
Isaiah 41:10 (ESV)

I had been struggling and needed success in my life. I also needed
love and direction. As I was contemplating this, these words
popped into my head—*You can do it*—followed by *I can help you*.
You know it was not I speaking, so it must have been the Lord. This
happened when I was in college. I realized that many of life's major
decisions are made during these formative years.

Let Jesus guide your footsteps, give you the will-power and
strength to push through your fears. I had asked friends, family and
strangers, but never the Lord. What a revelation!

My friend Joyce, a believer, along with Youth for Christ, lovingly
led me to the knowledge and life-saving grace of Jesus Christ. My
life has been changed forever!

Jesus is with you and me, and I know we can overcome. He is
our foundation, holding us up and keeping us strong. No matter the
distance between us, Christ is right beside you now. "I have chosen
you and have not rejected you" (Isaiah 41:9, NASB).

Challenge: Sometimes life is not the way we planned it, but Christ
can help redirect you and make you strong. Re-read Isaiah 41:10.

Prayer: Lord, I pray that You will help me and guide my footsteps.

Love always,
Grandma, Aunt Lynne and friend

Change Is Good

"Jesus is the same yesterday and today."
Hebrews 13:8 (NIV)

I s your life now in a state of change? Do you feel a little off balance? We ALL experience this at some point. Do not feel troubled and dismayed. God is in control! "Give thanks in all circumstances; for this is God's will for you in Christ Jesus" (1 Thessalonians 5:18, NIV).

Pray for each other. This can be your strength.

The choice is yours, renewal or the blues. Counselors are also helpful. Strive to become more like Christ. May learning be a joy rather than a chore. May you have clarity of mind, the ability to concentrate and the recollection of what has been learned. Along with my prayers, I ask God to put His everlasting arms around you to bring you comfort. Remember you can say, *I am not where I need to be, but I thank God I am not where I used to be*.

Challenge: Let God be in control so change may become easier. Change can be a blessing and exciting.

Prayer: I close my eyes remembering Your arms are around me and I feel comforted.

Love always,
Grandma, Aunt Lynne and friend

I Am Your Number One Fan, So Be Yourself

"I will pour out a blessing so great you won't have enough room to take it in!"
Malachi 3:10 (NLT)

" Each has his own gift from God!" (1 Corinthians 7:7, ESV). Do not be something you are not. Be yourself. You are empowered to perform the tasks God has given you on earth, so enjoy what He has for you or will call you to be. Do not fear.

He does not call on those who do not know and love Him. He is the enabler, but do good and share His blessings so others will give Him glory and honor.

Challenge: Thank God for your journey and the gifts and talents He has given you and will continue to give you. Do not long for someone else's gifts. May Christ dwell in those around you and the Spirit of God abide in you always.

Prayer: Help me be the unique person You have called me to be. Yes, there is more! I am special. Yes, I am special! Thanks be to God!

Love always,
Grandma, Aunt Lynne and friend

Praying the Scriptures

"I can do all things through Christ who strengthens me."
Philippians 4:13 (NKJV)

Philippians 4:13 can be your life verse. Proverbs 3:5-6 says, "Trust in the Lord with all your heart; and lean not unto your own understanding; in all your ways acknowledge Him, and He shall direct your paths" (NKJV). These two verses can serve in any situation no matter what, and the more you memorize by heart, the closer you are to the thousands of promises in the Bible.

These promises are potent, ones we can use to pray the Scriptures. My daughter-in-law tells me when I pray for her it is like praying the Scriptures. It can be the perfect prayer. God's Word is powerful, and you cannot go wrong.

Challenge: Put the verses on your board and challenge yourself to read them every day. This adds power to your walk and power to your talk.

Prayer: God, you are my God and my King. As I grow in grace and the light of Your love, help me to stand stronger than ever with the Word of God for what is right. I proclaim my life verse today.

Love always,
Grandma, Aunt Lynne and friend

Turn Ashes into Beauty

"Sorrow and mourning will disappear, and they will be
filled with joy and gladness."
Isaiah 51:11 (NLT)

Today I woke up with a terrible headache. Then I started praying the Scriptures without knowing the references. I am sure God does not mind.

The first verse I learned in college was "Be still, and know that I am God" (Psalm 46:10, ESV). Think about it and do it. "I can do all things through Christ who strengthens me" (Philippians 4:13, NKJV). "God causes all things to work together for good to those who love God" (Romans 8:28, NASB). "For in this hope we were saved. But hope that is seen is no hope at all. Who hopes for what they already have?" (Romans 8:24, NIV). Scripture has become my source and food for nourishment, especially in times of need.

Challenge: Turn to the Word in times of need to find Scripture that will encourage and strengthen you.

Prayer: I praise You, God. I love You. I glorify Your holy name. I look forward to what You have for me! Guide me for tomorrow, for today and for this moment! Take my hand and walk with me today, like Jesus carrying me with only one set of footprints in the sand.

Love always,
Grandma, Aunt Lynne and friend

I Am So Proud of You

"I take great pride in you."
2 Corinthians 7:4 (NIV)

Y ou are so special, and I want you to know how proud I am of you. To some, this year has been a struggle, and I commend you for all you have accomplished. To the rest of you, congratulations for soaring like eagles.

I have such a love and concern for you all and will pray for you throughout this year. Life can be special if you put God first on your list. If you do, things will fall into place. It can be a growing time both emotionally and physically. God is so good, and this time can be light and not darkness.

Challenge: Remember to continue to memorize the Scriptures, and you will be blessed. It is a good thing. Remember to "pray for one another so that you may be healed" (James 5:16, NASB). Also, have fun!

Prayer: God, I believe You are with me. I will take one step forward and claim this promise.

Love always,
Grandma, Aunt Lynne and friend

Life-Changing Prayer

"We continually ask God to fill you with the knowledge of his will
through all the wisdom and understanding that the Spirit gives, so that
you may live a life worthy of the Lord and please him in every way:
bearing fruit in every good work, growing in the knowledge of God,
being strengthened with all power according to his glorious might so that
you may have great endurance and patience."
Colossians 1:9-11 (NIV)

M y husband started taking notes when we were watching
Charles Stanley on TV. I challenge you to read Colossians
1:9-11. The following are excerpts and comments:

God will "fill you with the knowledge of His will" (Colossians
1:9, NIV); a sense of direction to spend your life knowing God to
walk in a manner (consistent conduct and character) worthy of Jesus
Christ and who He is. This is pleasing to God. Your goal is to follow
Him, living a life worthy of the Lord. "For we are God's workman-
ship, created in Christ Jesus to do good works, which God prepared
for us to do" (Ephesians 2:10, ESV).

"Being strengthened with all power" (Colossians 1:11, NIV).
Being filled with the Holy Spirit so that you will "hunger and thirst
after righteousness" (Matthew 5:6, KJV), so that you might by
His might grow in the knowledge of God (Colossians 1:10, NIV).
Bearing fruit of great endurance and patience in every good work
(Colossians 1:10-11, paraphrased).

Read the words, or are you just too busy? This is not acceptable.
Be productive in His will. Galatians 5:22-23 lists the fruit of the
Spirit: "Love, joy, peace, patience, kindness, goodness, faithfulness,
gentleness, and self-control" (NLT).

Since we live by the Spirit, let us keep in step with the Spirit.
"For it is not by grace you have been saved, through faith—and this
is not from yourselves, it is a gift of God—not by works, so that no
one can boast" (Ephesians 2:8-9, NIV).

Challenge: I have used many Bible translations and have concluded the Word and Living Waters are true and lasting. If you are thirsty, drink and be satisfied. Learn to study and then study some more!

Prayer: I come beside the still waters to drink, and I am filled with Your presence.

Love always,
Grandma, Aunt Lynne and friend

Cry to Me

"Will you not from this time cry to Me, 'My Father,
You are the guide of my youth?'"
Jeremiah 3:4 (NKJV)

As I write this, I think of all the years that my father, like his before him, was not the loving person he became in his later years when he had dementia.

Those years were filled with rage and absence and a person who didn't show his love to me. I begged for his love, and it just was not there. I felt abused, rejected, alone.

When I was forty I heard for the first time Dad saying, "Heavenly Father!" I knew then that he, by osmosis, had literally soaked up the presence of Christ in our hearts and our home.

Then when I was forty he said, "I love you!" I knew Dad was filled with God because he acknowledged Christ as Lord of his life.

All the years of emotional abuse started to dim, and he became the earthly father any daughter would long for.

So, my friend, God can heal a broken heart and fill a broken man with the greatest love of all, the eternal love of God.

God is real, God is good, and God is love! I hope you find hope!

Challenge: Trust God to change your circumstances and allow His love to fill your life. Give God any longing you may have for love from an earthly father, as you come to know the perfect love of your Heavenly and eternal Father

Prayer: God, I long for a loving and strong relationship with my earthly father. Because of Your love, I know this can happen.

Love always,
Grandma, Aunt Lynne and friend

Go Forth in the Name of Jesus

"Having loved his own who were in the world, he loved them to the end."
John 13:1 (NIV)

I dedicate this letter to Jesus, my living Savior and God. This being another year of writing letters finds our family and friends scattered. Because of God's presence in our lives it is much easier to pray and remember you as Christ remembers us.

God has given me blessings and love for you all. Our prayers should be remembered as circumstances vary. So go forth knowing Christ is with you. Remember that we will never have to face separation from Jesus' unfailing love.

Challenge: Memorizing Scripture should be your top priority. What you memorize today can be food for your spirit for the rest of your life. Just think if you are sick, stranded or alone. God is always with you in spirit and in truth.

Prayer: God, please touch each and every one as they venture with Your prayers and guidance. Let them know how special they are. I lift them up in the name of Jesus.

Love always,
Grandma, Aunt Lynne and friend

One More Note

It has been such a blessing to work with Lynne Granger and Bill Coté on this book and to assist in editing and proofreading. When Lynne asked me to share something I have learned in my walk with God, I thought of Peter. When Peter sees Jesus on the water, he inquires of the Lord, not knowing if it is He.

"'Lord, if it's you,' Peter replied, 'tell me to come to you on the water.' 'Come,' he said. Then Peter got down out of the boat, walked on the water and came toward Jesus." (Matthew 14:28-29, NIV).

Sometimes we are unsure of whether the Lord is calling us to do something. I recall several times throughout my life when I perhaps felt God nudging me to do something, but then I became unsure or even felt fearful of what the outcome might be.

One particular incident was right before I decided to participate in a seven-month mission-training program with Youth With a Mission (YWAM) in Germany. I had felt the initial call to go, had applied and even been accepted into the program, until fear and anxiety began to grip me. I second-guessed what God had spoken and starting thinking of all the reasons why I shouldn't go. I even waited on giving my professional job notice because I thought I might change my mind.

In the end, God made it very clear I was to go and even reminded me of the story of Esther. Many of us are called to do things "for such a time as this" (Esther 4:14). We never know how saying yes to God will affect others or even our own lives. You could change the course of someone else's life by your simple act of obedience.

I encourage you to read the story of Esther and ask God to show you how your life can change the world. Be willing to say yes!

God wanted me to "get out of the boat" like Peter. He gave me strength to do what He called me to, and I believe He gives strength for all of us to follow Him in faith.

With love in Christ,

Kate Luce

Afterword

"For I am the Lord your God, who stirs up the sea, causing His waves to
roar with living waters. Praise be to the Lord."
Isaiah 51:15 (NLT)

My word these last two years is hope. Would you like to be overflowing with hope and be in the hand of God?

It is so easy! Jesus died for you, and He forgives your sins, your deepest, darkest secrets. He then adds light to the package with a wonderful plan for your life. He is there to give you strength and guidance, so turn to Him.

Open up the best present of your life. It is a free gift of eternal life where your sins will be no more. "He will wipe every tear from their eyes. There will be no more death or mourning or crying or pain, for the old order of things has passed away" (Revelation 21:4, NIV).

Revelation 21:5 says, "To all who are thirsty, I will give freely from the springs of the water of life" (NLT). These are the springs of the Living Waters.

Original painting by Lynne Granger

Endnotes

1   Dan Wolgemuth, Youth for Christ, USA, personal letter

2   Merriam-Webster Online Dictionary <www.merriam-webster.com/dictionary/stewardship> accessed 12/29/2014

3   *The Normal Christian Life* by Watchman Nee (p. 100 cited in Google eBook, pages displayed by permission CLC Publications)

http://books.google.com/books?id=As25ZzScj4sC&pg=PT80&lpg=PT80&dq=the+path+of+every+Christian+has+been+clearly+marked+out+by+God,+and+it+is+of+supreme+importance+that+each+one+should+know+and+walk+in+the+God-appointed+course&source=bl&ots=7B0KKfd3gA&sig=YCWBtJqpgH6k25XXA-mot-x8nF5U&hl=en&sa=X&ei=_qGAVNnYCpP-yQTJ_4GYBg&ved=0CCYQ6AEwAQ#v=onepage&q=the%20path%20of%20every%20Christian%20has%20been%20clearly%20marked%20out%20by%20God%2C%20and%20it%20is%20of%20supreme%20importance%20that%20each%20one%20should%20know%20and%20walk%20in%20the%20God-appointed%20course&f=false CLC Publications 2012 www.clc-publications.com

4   *I Declare: 31 Promises to Speak over Your Life* by Joel Osteen FaithWords, Hachette Book Group, 2012 (cites p. 7)

5   *I Declare: 31 Promises to Speak over Your Life* by Joel Osteen
    FaithWords, Hachette Book Group, 2012. (not direct quote, just
    inspired)

6   *Instinct* by T. D. Jakes FaithWords, Hachette Book Group, 2014
    (not direct quote, just inspired)

7   *Instinct* by T. D. Jakes FaithWords, Hachette Book Group, 2014
    (not direct quote, paraphrased)

8   *Instinct* by T. D. Jakes FaithWords, Hachette Book Group, 2014,
    (not direct quote, paraphrased)

9   *9 Ways to Let Go of Stuck Thoughts* by Therese
    Borchard, May 13, 2014 http://thereseborchardblog.
    com/2014/05/13/9-ways-to-let-of-stuck-thoughts/
    "Stuck thoughts ... the brick walls that form a prison around
    your mind. The harder you try to get rid of them, the more pow-
    erful they become." (Above quote as appears on Bochard's blog.
    Added material appears in brackets in prayer letter within the text)

10 *Instinct* by T. D. Jakes FaithWords, Hachette Book Group, 2014
    (not direct quote, paraphrased)

11 *Instinct* by T. D. Jakes FaithWords, Hachette Book Group, 2014
    (not direct quote, paraphrased)

12 *Instinct* by T. D. Jakes FaithWords, Hachette Book Group, 2014
    (inspired by pg. 24-27)

13 *The Practice of the Presence of God* by Brother Lawrence
    (paperback) Benton Classics, Benton Publishing Group, 2013
    www.bentonpress.com (general concept paraphrased)

14 *Instinct* by T. D. Jakes FaithWords, Hachette Book Group, 2014
    (not direct quote, just inspired)

CPSIA information can be obtained
at www.ICGtesting.com
Printed in the USA
BVOW11s0307090616

451310BV00002B/2/P